JOSEPH STALIN
RUSSIA'S LAST CZAR

BY STEVEN OTFINOSKI

The Millbrook Press / Brookfield, Connecticut

Library of Congress Cataloging-in-Publication Data
Otfinoski, Steven.
Joseph Stalin : Russia's last czar / by Steven Otfinoski.
p.   cm.
Includes bibliographical references and index.
Summary: A biography of the Soviet dictator, who, under the guise
of communism and reform of a discontented society, was responsible
for the murder of fifty million people and incalculable suffering by
his countrymen.
ISBN 1-56294-240-9
1. Stalin, Joseph, 1879–1953—Juvenile literature.   2. Heads of
state—Soviet Union—Biography—Juvenile literature.   3. Soviet
Union—History—1925–1953—Juvenile literature.   [1. Stalin,
Joseph, 1879–1953.   2. Heads of state.   3. Soviet Union—
History—1925–1953.]   I. Title.
DK268.S8O88   1993
947.084'2'092—dc20   [B]   92-41143   CIP   AC

Photos courtesy of: UPI/Bettmann: pp. 2, 11, 18, 21, 38,
71, 77, 82, 84, 89, 97, 105; New York Public Library Picture
Collection: pp. 28, 41; The Bettmann Archive: pp. 48, 102;
Culver Pictures: pp. 54, 60, 111.

Map by Frank Senyk

Published by The Millbrook Press
2 Old New Milford Road, Brookfield, Connecticut 06804

ONTENTS

JOSEPH STALIN

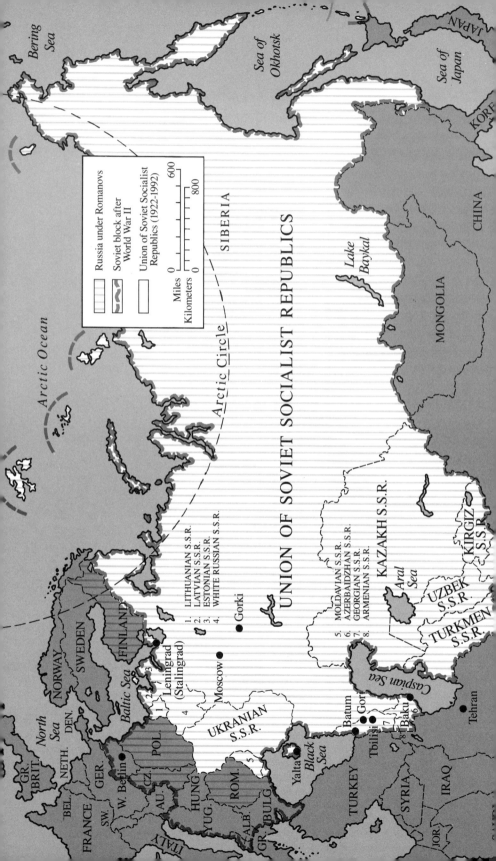

Bering
Sea

Sea of
Okhotsk

Sea of
Japan

JAPAN

KOREA

CHINA

MONGOLIA

SIBERIA

Lake
Baykal

Arctic Ocean

Arctic Circle

UNION OF SOVIET SOCIALIST REPUBLICS

Russia under Romanovs
Soviet block after World War II
Union of Soviet Socialist Republics (1922-1992)

Miles
Kilometers

0   600
0   800

1. LITHUANIAN S.S.R.
2. LATVIAN S.S.R.
3. ESTONIAN S.S.R.
4. WHITE RUSSIAN S.S.R.

5. MOLDAVIAN S.S.R.
6. AZERBAIDZHAN S.S.R.
7. GEORGIAN S.S.R.
8. ARMENIAN S.S.R.

KAZAKH S.S.R.

KIRGIZ S.S.R.

UZBEK S.S.R.

TURKMEN S.S.R.

Aral
Sea

• Gorki

• Moscow

Leningrad
(Stalingrad)

Baltic Sea

FINLAND

SWEDEN

NORWAY

DEN.

North
Sea

GR.
BRIT.

NETH.

BEL.

GER.

W. Berlin

FRANCE

SW.

AU.

POL.

CZ.

HUNG.

ITALY

YUG.

ROM.

ALB.

GR.

BULG.

UKRANIAN
S.S.R.

Yalta

Black
Sea

Batum

Gori

Tbilisi

Caspian Sea

Baku

Tehran

TURKEY

SYRIA

IRAQ

JOR.

1
TWO
GHOSTS

ON A COLD, CRISP MOSCOW NIGHT in October 1961, a corpse was buried without ceremony outside the wall of the Kremlin, Russia's age-old seat of government. The grave site was a quiet spot, surrounded by fir and yew trees. A plain, brown coffin containing a well-preserved body was placed into a pit. The pit was then filled with tons of cement—having moved the body once, the Soviet government had no intention of moving it again. A few weeks later, a slab of polished granite was placed on top of the grave. It read simply:

J. V. STALIN

Thus the man who had ruled the world's largest nation for more than a quarter century came to his final resting place—a corpse encased in cement.

The complicated process of "destalinization" that culminated in this bizarre burial had begun at the 20th Congress of the Communist party in February 1956. Nikita Khrushchev, party secretary and Stalin's heir, had stunned the 1,500 delegates in the Great Hall of the Kremlin Palace with a blistering denunciation of the man who had raised him to power.

Referring to the persecution of innocent members of the party, Khrushchev said, "In a whole series of cases, Stalin showed his intolerance, his brutality and his abuse of power. . . . Comrades! We must abolish the cult of personality decisively, once and for all." [1]

The 20,000-word speech, like the burial that followed five years later, was kept secret from the public. While it was read at party meetings across the Soviet Union, not a word of Khrushchev's speech was published in the press. Yet people knew. Within twenty-four hours of the address, Moscow was buzzing with the news that the

Stalin's grave by the Kremlin wall in December 1964, three years after his body was removed from Lenin's mausoleum. The flowers were left by three anonymous admirers to commemorate the 85th anniversary of the dictator's birth.

man who had been a demigod for decades was now a national pariah.

Throughout the Soviet bloc of Eastern Europe, portraits of Stalin were pulled from shop windows and government buildings. Statues were melted down. Streets, towns, and cities were renamed. The city of Stalingrad, the late dictator's pride and joy, was rechristened Volgograd. The image and name of the great Stalin, the Father of the Peoples, the Transformer of Nature, all but disappeared from the face of the empire.

Only one persistent image remained—the man himself. His body, carefully preserved by a secret embalming compound, lay on a bier in the Kremlin mausoleum alongside a man Stalin had loved, served, and betrayed—Vladimir Lenin.

At the 22nd Party Congress in the fall of 1961, Khrushchev led the heated debate over what to do with Stalin's body. A ghostly figure from the distant Bolshevik past became Khrushchev's most eloquent advocate for its removal.

Her name was Dora Abramovna Lazurkina. She was a frail survivor from a time that was a dim memory to most living Soviets. Lazurkina was one of the original circle of Bolsheviks who had followed Lenin to victory in the Russian Revolution of 1917. She was one of the last links with the revolutionary past, a time of great hopes, that had been dashed when Stalin took over the reins of power and changed Russia forever. During the purges of the 1930s, Lazurkina had been arrested and had spent seventeen years in prison and labor camps. Somehow she had managed to survive the long ordeal that had claimed the lives of nearly all her comrades.

Now, here she stood in the Great Hall, this frail but flinty woman in a simple black dress, to give her testimony for posterity. And what testimony it was! A living ghost herself, Lazurkina claimed to spend much of her time conversing with the ghost of Lenin. A hush fell over the Great Hall as Dora Lazurkina spoke of her latest communication with the Father of Soviet Communism.

"Yesterday I consulted him," she told the Congress in a shrill, insistent voice. "He was standing there before me as if he were alive, and he said: 'It is unpleasant to be next to Stalin, who did so much harm to the party.' "[2]

Lenin's testimony, even once removed, could not be ignored. After Lazurkina spoke, Khrushchev read the final decree. Stalin's continued presence in Lenin's tomb was "inappropriate since the serious violations by Stalin of Lenin's precepts, abuse of power, mass repressions against honorable Soviet people, and other activities in the period of the personality cult make it impossible to leave the bier with his body in the mausoleum of V. I. Lenin."[3]

Within the month, Stalin was laid in his final resting place. Or was he? For those superstitious Muscovites who believed in real ghosts, Stalin's spirit was surely capable of rising again. Not even six feet of concrete was protection against the "man of steel."

In the age of *perestroika* and *glasnost*—economic change and a new openness in Soviet society—Stalin's ghost continued to haunt the Kremlin. Even after Soviet communism died in 1991, there were those in the former Soviet Union who longed for Stalin's return. Others, who had clearer memories of what Russia was like under Stalin, gazed on his lonely grave near the Kremlin wall and shuddered.

To exorcise Stalin's ghost from our world, we must not cover his memory with concrete, but examine it closely. We must come to grips with the fact that this terrible tyrant was also a creator who, with an iron will, industrialized a backward, agricultural society and turned it into one of the most powerful countries on earth. Only when we understand both Stalin's achievements and what they cost the Soviet people will we be able to put his ghost to rest once and for all.

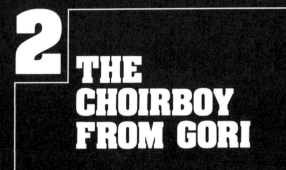

2 THE CHOIRBOY FROM GORI

I know my son rules in the Kremlin,
but if he had not been naughty
and turned away from God and
been forced to leave his school
he might by now be a bishop.

Ekaterina Dzhugashvili,
Stalin's mother[1]

OF THE FIFTEEN REPUBLICS that make up the former Soviet Union, few have as rich and fascinating a past as Georgia. Tucked away in the southwestern corner of Russia, between the Black and Caspian seas, Georgia lies at the crossroads of two continents—Europe and Asia. An independent state since it became Christian in the fourth century, Georgia remained free until 1801, when its last king submitted to Russia, its giant neighbor to the north.

Georgia is a land of sharp contrasts. A fertile region of great natural beauty, it has a long history of violent, dark deeds. Blood feuds between families can last for generations, taking many lives. Serfdom, a form of feudal bondage, was not abolished there until nearly two decades after it vanished from the rest of Russia. This beautiful wild land—half European, half Asian—was the birthplace of one of the most ruthless tyrants of the twentieth century.

Iosif Vissarionovich Dzhugashvili, later to become Joseph Stalin, was born in the Georgian village of Gori four days before Christmas in 1879. He was named for Saint Joseph by his deeply religious mother, who prayed that he would survive infancy. She had good reason to pray. Her two previous children had died soon after birth. Ekaterina Dzhugashvili felt her prayers had been answered. Little Soso, Russian for Joey, lived—her only surviving child.

Gori was a peaceful village, famous for its sweet apples, golden wine, and cotton fields. But there was no peace for Soso's father, Vissarion Ivanovich Dzhugashvili. He was a brooding, violent man who barely made a living as a shoemaker. The family lived in a squalid two-room shack on a dirt road often wet with raw sewage. Disease, degradation, and death were a daily part of their lives.

At seven, Soso caught smallpox and nearly died. The disease left his face scarred for life. But other scars—psychological ones—would disfigure the boy in far worse ways. When drunk, his father would beat him mercilessly. A beating may have caused another deformity. An injury to the boy's left arm went unattended and led to blood poisoning. Soso survived, but his left arm was three inches shorter than his right, and he never had full use of his left hand again.

The boy came to hate his father intensely. Once he hurled a knife at him to defend his mother, who also was a victim of Vissarion's brutality. The knife missed, and Soso ran away to live with a neighbor for a time. When the boy was ten, his father died, as violently as he had lived, in a tavern brawl. If it were not for his mother's love and determination, Soso might easily have followed his father's path of dissolution to an early death.

But Ekaterina was determined that her beloved son would amount to something. She sent him to the village church school, using the money she earned by working as a domestic in the homes of well-to-do people. Soso was a good student with a quick mind. He loved to read, especially stories of adventure. Yet learning and ideas, for their own sake, did not matter much to him. Education would always be a means to an end—in this case, getting out of Gori. He was not, and never would be, an intellectual.

There was only one route of escape from the miserable lot of a poor cobbler's son in this backwater of the Russian Empire, and that was religion. Ekaterina's great ambition for her son was the priesthood. A priest of the Orthodox Church was the most respected member of peasant society.

As a young boy, Soso shared his mother's deep Christian faith. He truly enjoyed church. The Georgian Orthodox Church was a magical place for him. The service with its elaborate liturgy, choral singing, and long-bearded patriarchs lifted him out of his dingy life to a higher realm. He had a good voice and became a choirboy. He even sang a solo on the birthday of Czar Alexander III.

When Soso graduated from school at the top of his class, he received a small scholarship to the Theological Seminary in Tbilisi,* the Georgian capital 30 miles (48 kilometers) away. His mother's fondest dream was coming true. Her little Soso was to become a priest.

* The name of the city in Stalin's day was spelled Tiflis. The modern spelling will be used here.

The seminary, however, was not the ivory tower of learning she imagined it to be. It reflected the world of czarist Russia, and that world was not a pretty one. Georgia chafed under the heavy yoke of its Russian masters. Russian bureaucrats ran the government, the church, and the educational system. The only schools allowed to operate in Georgia were those run by the church, which was merely an arm of the czarist state. Georgian language, literature, and culture were stricken from the curriculum.

The administration at the Tbilisi Seminary wielded religion as a weapon over their students, pounding them into submission with its repressive weight. Students were forced to stand through long services. Curfews were strictly enforced. Books containing any criticism of society were forbidden. The slightest infringement of the rules resulted in harsh punishment. Stalin's childhood friend Joseph Iremashvili, who later wrote a book about him, described the school this way:

> *The atmosphere was dull and oppressive. There was scarcely any expression of youthful joy, hemmed in as we were by rooms and corridors which cut us off from the outside world. When, as happened from time to time, we gave expression to our youthful temperaments, we were quickly suppressed by the monks and monitors.* [2]

Like Tbilisi itself, which served as a dumping ground for dissidents from all over Russia, the seminary became a hotbed of revolutionary activity. A few years before Soso's arrival, a student had actually shot and killed the school's Russian principal, who had publicly denounced all things Georgian. The student was hanged by the government and became a martyred hero in his homeland.

At first Soso was not touched by this radical element. He excelled at his studies and caused little trouble. His feelings of nationalism were expressed in poetry, for which he developed a passion. The man who would one day censor all artistic expression in his country possessed a modest lyrical gift. A number of his poems were published in small literary magazines. Here is Stalin's first published poem, written when he was fifteen:

MORNING

The rose opens petals,
And embraces the violet.
The lily too has awakened.
They bend their heads to the zephyrs.

The lark climbs high in the sky
And sings his ringing song:
The nightingale with subtle voice
Sings softly on:

"Flourish, O adorable country,
Rejoice, O land of Iveria,*
And you also, O learned men of Georgia,
May you bring joy and happiness to the country!"3

Soso's youthful sensitivity would soon fade. The Tbilisi Theological Seminary would see to that. The young Dzhugashvili hardened under its tutelage. He learned to hate religion and all authority. But he also learned how to survive in this hostile environment. He became devious, hiding his true feelings behind a mask of hypocrisy. He met secretly with his fellow students after curfew to conspire against the administration. He read Karl Marx's *Das*

---

* Iveria is the ancient name for Georgia.

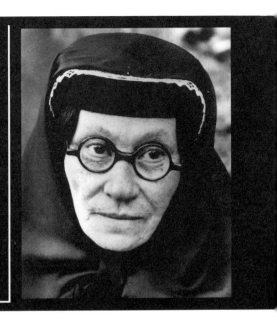

Stalin's mother, Ekaterina Djugashvili, posed for this portrait only a few years before her death in 1936. It was her determination and hard-earned money that pushed her son into the seminary. A deeply religious woman, she never got over her disappointment that her "Soso" became a revolutionary instead of a priest.

Kapital, a condemnation of the capitalist system, behind the cover of a prayer book in chapel.

Stalin was not alone in his fascination with Marx's writings. Marx's ideas were being taken up by disenchanted intellectuals and revolutionaries throughout the country. Marx believed that history was a series of class conflicts and that the capitalist system was inherently corrupt and unjust. Under his new order of communism, he believed the workers of the world, whom he called the proletariat, would rise up against the money-grubbing middle class and overthrow it. Then the proletariat would create a classless society where personal property would be abolished and all citizens would be equal.

In 1898 the Russian Social Democratic Labor party was founded on the principles of Marxist thought. Marxism, however, was not the first radical movement in Russia. Throughout much of the nineteenth century, socialist and populist groups called for radical reform, while anarchists and terrorists committed violent acts and assassinations in attempts to overthrow the czarist government.

Soso, along with other seminarians, attended Social Democratic meetings in the homes of local workers. It wasn't long before he became a member of the Tbilisi chapter of the party.

As he became more involved in the revolutionary underground, Soso abandoned all thoughts of becoming a priest. However, he remained at school, with the vague ambition of getting a job as a teacher after graduation to support himself. His last summer vacation in Tbilisi changed his mind. Spreading the gospel of Karl Marx among the working-class people of the city gave the insecure young man a sense of power and mission that he had never known before. As a follower of Marx, Soso gained the respect and self-confidence he so desperately needed. Personal ambition and hatred for the ruling class drove him on, not love for the masses. In the years ahead these qualities would set him apart from his revolutionary colleagues and ultimately be the source of his power.

When Soso returned to the seminary in the fall of 1898, he had lost all interest in his studies. He began to fail his courses, and his insolent behavior got him into more and more trouble. In his conduct book an assistant supervisor wrote, "Dzhugashvili is genuinely disrespectful and rude toward persons in authority and systematically refuses to bow to one of the masters, as the latter has repeatedly complained to the board of supervision."[4]

A week from the end of his five-year course, Joseph Dzhugashvili was expelled from the seminary after missing his exams. His mother was heartbroken. Her high hopes for her Soso were dashed. But for the nineteen-year-old boy with the cruel brown eyes, life was just beginning. He had found his true vocation in life—that of a revolutionary.

3

CODE NAME KOBA

A new class has entered the arena— the proletariat.

Stalin, in an article in the journal *Brdzola* (The Struggle), 1904[1]

AS THE NINETEENTH CENTURY drew to a close, Russia was a country ripe for revolution. Discontent and frustration had been simmering under the country's placid surface for decades. Within the next five years, the people's anger would reach a boiling point. Like many European countries, Russia had been under the rule of absolute monarchs for centuries. But unlike such countries as France and England, Russia's kings, the czars, had not been overthrown by revolution or tempered by reform. The Romanov dynasty had ruled since 1613 over a vast empire that included not only Russia but a dozen other countries with various ethnic backgrounds. Like the Georgians, the peoples of these lands yearned for independence from czarist Russia.

The Romanovs had kept Russia isolated, largely out of touch with the rest of Western civilization. Progress was slow, and four fifths of the population lived much as their distant forefathers had, tending small farms in tiny villages that dotted the vast countryside. The Industrial Revolution got a late start in Russia, and the lives of workers in city factories were every bit as miserable as those of the peasant farmers. Attempts at reform, such as the abolishment of serfdom in 1861, only fueled the fires of discontent. The 1860s saw the growth of organized protests and demonstrations against the government. The assassination of government leaders became commonplace. Czar Alexander II himself was killed by a terrorist's bomb in 1881.

The Marxist-inspired Social Democratic Labor party may have been just one of many outlawed political organizations, but it boasted one of the most dynamic of revolutionary leaders, Vladimir I. Lenin. Lenin, the son of a middle-ranking bureaucrat, had been exiled to Siberia in

1897, but moved to Switzerland in 1900 upon his release. There he founded the revolutionary journal *Iskra* (The Spark). For all but three of the next seventeen years, Lenin would conduct his revolutionary activities from abroad.

Young Dzhugashvili left the Tbilisi Theological Seminary ready to work wholeheartedly for the Social Democrats, but he needed money to support himself. He got a job—one of the few "regular" jobs he ever held—working as a clerk at the Tbilisi Geophysical Observatory. Stalin later claimed he spent his time making important astronomical observations. In reality, he was probably little more than a bookkeeper. One of the first things Stalin did once he achieved supreme power in the late 1920s was to completely revise his personal history to exaggerate his early achievements. He did the job well. Even in the age of *glasnost*, the facts of Stalin's early life are still shadowy.

We do know that his first active role as a member of the Social Democratic party was as an organizer of a May Day demonstration in 1900 outside Tbilisi. It was also the first time Stalin spoke in public, although he seems to have made little impression on his audience. Unlike Lenin, Trotsky, and other leading revolutionaries, Stalin was not a gifted orator. He spoke haltingly with a thick Georgian accent that stayed with him all his life. Stalin's power would lie more in action than in words.

In March 1901 the czar's secret police, the dreaded Okhranka, cracked down on revolutionaries in the Georgian capital. They began rounding up all known Social Democrats. Stalin managed to escape their dragnet, but his room was searched and put under surveillance. He began living the life of a hunted man, sleeping by day and moving around by night. He wore elaborate disguises to escape arrest and adopted a number of aliases to confuse the police. He was known as David, Kato, and Ivanovich among other names. But the alias Stalin was most fond of came from one of his favorite childhood books.

At thirteen, Stalin had read a novel about the legendary Georgian bandit Koba. Koba was a ruthless outlaw whose only loyalty was to his native Georgia, where he was considered a hero. There is no doubt that Stalin saw himself as a modern-day Koba, fighting for his people against the czarist government. Like his hero, Stalin was ruthless, cunning, and a loner. But in one respect he was nothing at all like Koba. Stalin had little personal courage. He loved to stir up trouble, to incite a crowd, or to start a riot. But when violence broke out, Stalin was nowhere to be found.

In his very first published article, "The Russian Social Democratic Party and Its Immediate Tasks," Stalin put forth the disturbing idea that violence was good, especially if innocent bystanders were hurt. Bloodshed brought sympathy to the revolutionaries and made new converts to their cause.

Such ruthlessness appalled Stalin's colleagues in the party. But Stalin was hardly concerned about what his fellow revolutionaries thought of him. He took perverse pleasure in dividing party members against each other and spreading discord in the ranks. This destructive behavior weakened his rivals and made him stronger. After two years of Stalin's subversive behavior, the Tbilisi Social Democrats had had enough. They forced him out of the party and told him to leave Tbilisi.

In November 1901 the young, footloose revolutionary moved to Batum, a Georgian city on the Black Sea. Batum's major industry was oil drilled from the Black Sea. The workers in the oil refinery labored under brutal conditions and were ready to listen to this young revolutionary. Stalin organized a strike at the refinery that resulted in the firing of 400 men, many of whom were arrested. He then led a political demonstration outside the jail where many workers were imprisoned. The demonstration culminated in a giant rally where fifteen people were killed by police and many more wounded. Stalin had slipped away before the bloodshed started.

The Social Democrats in Batum were as unhappy with Stalin as their counterparts in Tbilisi had been. They also had reason to believe that he was an *agent provocateur*, a spy in the pay of the czar's police. From this distance in time it is impossible to say for certain if Stalin was a spy. But if he was, it would explain how he avoided arrest for so long, and why time after time he returned so easily from exile. It would also explain why years later Stalin was so obsessed with hiding his past. He might well have feared the world would learn that the leader of the Communist world had once been a paid informant in the employ of the czar!

Stalin was finally arrested by the police on April 18, 1902. For the next year and a half he sat in prison, waiting for his trial. Stalin was sentenced to exile in Siberia, a rite of passage for nearly every revolutionary of the day.

Exile in Siberia was not the horrible fate it might seem today. To be sure, Siberia was a remote, frozen wasteland. But it had towns and cities even then, and exiles were free to work and live more or less normal lives, although they were often closely watched by police. Some exiles even married and had families. When their sentence was up, they were free to return home, where they usually resumed their revolutionary activities.

While Stalin sat in Siberia, an event occurred within the Social Democratic party that was to have far-reaching effects on the revolutionary movement in Russia. The Social Democrats split into two distinct factions over the

Prison and exile were a way of life for the young revolutionary. Here Stalin is seen in police "mug shots" taken around 1913, probably following his last arrest. Rumors that he was a secret agent for the czarist police persist to this day.

issue of who would run the party. The Mensheviks* wanted to open party membership to the majority of Russians. The Bolsheviks, led by Lenin, wanted to limit party membership to a small group of devoted revolutionaries. Although he claimed to have the people's good at heart, Lenin believed only a small elite, the Bolshevik party, knew what was best for them and could effectively organize a revolution. This line of thought appealed immensely to Stalin. Power was what he wanted, and by joining the Bolsheviks he could become part of that power base. From that day forward, Lenin was Stalin's hero and role model.

---

* The word *Menshevik* means "minority" in Russian, but ironically the Mensheviks were a majority in the Social Democratic party at the time, while the *Bolsheviks* (meaning "majority") were a much smaller group.

After only two months in the remote Siberian village of Novaya Uda, Stalin tried to escape on foot, armed with a hunting rifle. Wolves drove him back the first time, but a second attempt succeeded.

Stalin returned to Tbilisi in 1904 and then went to Gori, where his mother hid him from the authorities. Her love for her only child had not diminished, despite her disappointment that he had turned away from God. At home, Stalin met a pretty Georgian girl, Ekaterina Svanidze, who was the sister of a friend from his seminary days. They married in 1904. Keke, as Stalin called her, was a traditional Georgian wife, totally submissive to her husband.

Stalin loved his wife with a warmth that was unknown in his relationships with anyone outside his family. Soon they had a son named Yakov. In his memoir, Stalin's old friend Iremashvili wrote, "Only his wife, his child and his mother were exempt from the scorn he poured out on everyone else."[2]

The year 1904 was a turning point in the history of modern Russia. The nation went to war against its imperialist rival, Japan. Czar Nicholas II saw the war as an opportunity to turn his people's attention away from discontent at home. By defeating Japan in the Japanese-occupied territory of Korea and Manchuria, Nicholas also hoped to extend his empire and brighten his tarnished reputation.

The Japanese were far better prepared for war than the Russians and launched a devastating surprise attack on the Russian fort at Port Arthur in Manchuria in February. After one humiliating defeat after another on land and at sea, the Russians were forced to the peace table in September 1905. The treaty gave the Japanese every advantage in the Far East and established them as a world power. The czar was shown as weak and vulnerable, and the Russian people seized the initiative to strike out against his corrupt government.

The Revolution of 1905 was led by neither the Bolsheviks nor the Mensheviks. It was a spontaneous uprising of the Russian people. On January 22, 1905, a simple priest led 200,000 unarmed striking workers to the Winter Palace in St. Petersburg, then the capital of Russia, to deliver a petition to the czar. They were met by government troops who opened fire on them. Hundreds of people were killed or wounded in what came to be called Bloody Sunday.

In response to further acts of insurrection and countless assassinations, the czar announced several reform measures, including the establishment of a parliament, called the Duma, and a new constitution. The brief revolution, however, effectively destroyed the people's faith in a good, fatherly czar and drove millions of workers into the arms of the revolutionaries who espoused violence as the only cure for tyranny.

St. Petersburg, where the Revolution started, gave birth to a council, or soviet, called the Soviet of Workers' Deputies. Its chairman was a high-ranking Menshevik, Leon Trotsky, who was later imprisoned for his part in the Revolution. A galvanizing speaker and formidable intellectual, Trotsky gave the rallying cry for all those who refused to give up their dream of a new Russia: "The Revolution is dead. Long live the Revolution!"[3]

Stalin characteristically stayed on the sidelines during the turmoil of 1905. But his writings and revolutionary work were gaining some attention in Tbilisi. At year-end he was sent by local party members to a secret Bolshevik conference in Finland. Here, Stalin came face to face for the first time with his hero, Lenin. Stalin later wrote his impression of this historic occasion: "I was expecting to see the mountain eagle of our party, a great man. . . . What was my disappointment when I saw the most ordinary-looking man, below middle height, distinguished from ordinary mortals by nothing, literally nothing."[4]

What is interesting about this assessment of Lenin is how closely it parallels descriptions of Stalin in later years by foreign visitors meeting him for the first time. Both men were not as impressive in person as their image in the media. On their next meeting, Lenin and Stalin would begin to take a truer measure of each other. Both would like what they saw.

4 THE ROAD TO REVOLUTION

Coarse and brutal, disrespectful to the authorities. Quarrels with the town folk. It is suggested that the Governor of Vologda should transfer him to the village of Kriouskooka.

Local police report
on Stalin in
Vyatka, Russia, 1909[1]

HE YEARS FROM 1906 to 1917 were ones of trial and tribulation for the young Stalin. He spent seven of those eleven years in prison or exile and most of the others hiding out from the police. Throughout all this adversity, he continued to write, speak, and promote himself within the Bolshevik party.

At a Social Democratic Congress in Stockholm, Sweden, in 1906, Stalin met Lenin a second time. Lenin found the young Georgian to be a refreshing change from many of the Bolsheviks in Lenin's circle, most of whom were intellectuals like Lenin himself. Stalin was a ruthless and hardheaded pragmatist, whom Lenin saw as the kind of down-to-earth fellow capable of winning over the different ethnic groups within Russia to the revolutionary cause.

Stalin wasted no time in proving his usefulness to his leader. The party needed money—lots of it—to promote its cause, and Lenin didn't care where it came from. Stalin returned to the Caucasus and gathered around him a band of professional thugs, thieves, and cutthroats. They staged a series of daring bank robberies, supplemented by a protection racket that extorted money from local businesses. The stores of those who didn't pay up on time were firebombed. The criminals took their share of the loot, and the rest went into the party's coffers.

If Lenin was pleased with Stalin's work, the Bolsheviks were not. Criminal activities were not part of their agenda for a revolution. Even Stalin's comrades in the Caucasus were ready to disown him after he masterminded a major robbery at the Imperial Bank in Tbilisi on June 25, 1907. Although Stalin escaped prosecution by the legal authorities, a Bolshevik tribunal found him guilty of being an independent agent and expelled him from their party.

It was not a good year for Stalin. His young wife died of an illness, possibly pneumonia, and he took it harder than any death in his life. "She was the one creature who softened my heart of stone," he confided to an old friend after the funeral. "She is dead, and with her have died my last warm feelings for humanity."[2] His actions over the next forty-five years would prove the truth of this statement with frightening accuracy.

The wandering revolutionary took to the road once more. He drifted to Baku, on the west coast of the Caspian Sea. Like Batum, Baku was a city built on oil. Stalin organized the oil workers there to strike and demonstrate and was arrested by the police in March 1908. It was back to prison, this time for seven and a half months. Bailov Prison might have been a loathsome place for the average revolutionary, but Stalin was in his element. Another prisoner later wrote that he "was always seen in the company of cutthroats, political blackmailers, robbers, and gun slingers."[3] Instead of befriending new Bolshevik arrivals, he falsely spread the word that they were spies and then sat back and watched the mayhem. His actions were responsible for the murder of at least one prisoner.

Many Bolshevik prisoners undoubtedly breathed easier when Stalin was sent into exile to Siberia in November. The two-year sentence was considered extremely mild for a convicted revolutionary and again raised questions of whether Stalin was a police spy himself. He escaped within months but was arrested again in March 1910 and returned to Siberia to serve out his two-year sentence.

On the last day of 1910, the exile wrote a letter to a Central Committee member that was meant for Lenin, then living in Paris. Stalin wrote:

The most important thing is to organize the work in Russia . . . around a strictly defined princi-

ple. . . . In my view our next task, which must not be delayed, is the organization of a central (Russian) group, which would coordinate the illegal, semilegal and legal work at first in the main centers. . . . Such a group is as necessary as air, as bread. . . . Now about myself I have another six months to serve. When the term expires, I shall be entirely at your service.[4]

The letter impressed Lenin. He too felt that the revolution had been discussed and debated abroad for too long. It needed to be directed within Russia itself by someone like this "wonderful Georgian" who had stayed the course, living by his wits, while other revolutionaries lived lives of comparative ease abroad.

Stalin was released from exile in June 1911. Lenin was now in Prague, Czechoslovakia, busy organizing his forces. At a conference in February 1912, he announced the formation of a separate, seven-member Central Committee that would govern the Bolshevik party. Two more names were later added to the Committee—a metalworker named Belostotsky and Joseph Dzhugashvili.

Stalin didn't learn of his appointment for another month and was delirious when he got the news. Part of Lenin's plan to energize the Bolsheviks was the establishment of a daily newspaper to disseminate party propaganda. Stalin was involved in the founding of *Pravda*, (Truth), a journal still in existence today. Stalin later claimed to have put out *Pravda*'s first issue almost single-handedly. In fact, he was one of twenty contributors.

On May 5, the same day *Pravda*'s first issue came out, Stalin was arrested and sentenced to three years in northwestern Siberia. He once more escaped and went to St. Petersburg. An obscure revolutionary only a year before, Stalin was now the second most important Bolshevik in the city. To celebrate his new status, he retired all his old aliases and came up with a new and permanent one. In January 1913, Dzhugashvili signed a magazine article Stalin, meaning "man of steel."

It was while visiting with Lenin in Vienna, Austria, that Stalin first met Leon Trotsky. Trotsky was no longer a Menshevik and was a close friend of Lenin's. Trotsky found Stalin boorish, crude, and malevolent. Stalin thought Trotsky arrogant, cold, and egotistical, and he was jealous of the more intimate relationship that Trotsky had with Lenin.

Soon after returning to St. Petersburg, Stalin was arrested again and exiled to Siberia for the sixth and last time. This time he would receive no leniency. If he had been a police informant, it is unlikely he was still an active one. He was sent to the village of Kureika above the Arctic Circle and 1,000 miles (1,600 kilometers) from the nearest large settlement. Kureika was so far north that nine months of the year it was in total darkness. Stalin spent his time hunting and trapping with a dog, Tishka, who became his only friend and companion.

While Stalin languished in the frozen north, earth-shaking events were taking place in Europe. World War I broke out in August 1914, and Russia was on the side of the Western Allies against Germany, the Austro-Hungarian Empire, and the Ottoman Empire. In the nine years since the end of the Russo-Japanese War, the czar had done his best to develop a powerful war machine, but he was still woefully unprepared to go up against the superior fighting power of Germany. The only resource he had in unending supply was men. Countless waves of Russian soldiers went to their deaths at the front.

By the end of 1916 defeat seemed inevitable for the

The suddenness of the Russian Revolution caught everyone by surprise. The unpopularity of World War I undoubtedly hastened the czar's downfall. Here, soldiers pause to brandish their sabers as they lead the people of Petrograd in a march on the Duma, or Parliament.

Russians. In despair, the czar drafted political exiles to fill the dwindling ranks. Stalin and his colleagues were ordered to travel by foot, reindeer sled, and finally train, to an induction center a thousand miles away. It appeared to have been a wasted journey for Stalin. He was rejected for service because he couldn't bend his deformed left elbow. But before he could start back to exile, the stunning news arrived that the czar had given up his throne. The 300-year-old Romanov dynasty was at an end.

It had happened with the suddenness of summer lightning. Discontentment on the home front had been heightened by food shortages and other hardships of a war that most Russians never wanted. Families of dead soldiers felt their real enemy wasn't Germany but their own repressive government. The people rose up, with the firm support of the liberal politicians in the Duma. They set up a provisional government opposed to the czar. Besieged by riots and strikes, Nicholas II stepped down. The coup was relatively bloodless; only 1,500 people were wounded or killed. The provisional government declared Russia a republic.

Everyone was taken by surprise, even the Bolsheviks. As Robert Payne has pointed out, "Never was there a revolution which needed the help of revolutionaries so little."[5] One of the first acts of the new government was the granting of amnesty to all political exiles. Stalin left immediately for Petrograd, formerly St. Petersburg.* He arrived there by train on March 25, 1917, with fellow exile and Central Committee member Lev Kamenev. Together they took over the production of *Pravda*.

Stalin was surprisingly cooperative with the liberals who ran the new government. He was also conciliatory with the Mensheviks and Social Revolutionaries who dominated the Petrograd workers' council. In his first post-revolutionary article in *Pravda*, Stalin declared: "Land for the peasants, protection of labor for the workers, and a democratic republic for all the citizens of Russia!"[6]

Lenin, unable to leave Switzerland because the war was raging all around him, saw such compromising as a betrayal of Bolshevik principles. He wrote his own articles

---

* The provisional government felt St. Petersburg sounded too German, so the city's name was changed to the more Russian Petrograd. Not long after it would become Leningrad. After the fall of communism, it became St. Petersburg once more.

that branded members of the provisional government as traitors in league with the czar. Stalin, who was uncertain about Lenin's role in the new Russia, edited his leader's articles, watering down their message.

Why did Stalin play along with his enemies? He probably believed that to survive, the Bolsheviks needed to go along with the provisional government, biding their time for a takeover.

Lenin was anxious to get back to Russia. He willingly accepted the help of the Germans, who felt that if they could help place Lenin in power, the Russians would withdraw from the war. The Germans arranged for him to travel across war-torn Europe in a sealed train from Switzerland to the Finland Station in Petrograd, where he arrived on April 3.

Thousands of workers and Bolsheviks were waiting to welcome Lenin home after his ten years of exile. He climbed on top of an armored car and gave a riveting speech, reminding the crowd that the Revolution had only begun. Stalin was conspicuously absent from the historic occasion. He knew Lenin was displeased with him and probably decided it would be more politic to keep a low profile.

While Lenin later took Stalin to task for collaborating with the provisional government, he did not demote him. Lenin knew the Bolsheviks, still a small minority, would need to stick together in the struggle ahead, and Stalin was the kind of man who could prove useful.

The provisional government's weak leadership became apparent as the country slowly sank into anarchy. Alexander Kerensky, head of the provisional government, scheduled elections for a Constituent Assembly on November 12. At an October 23 meeting of the Central Committee, Lenin announced his plan for a Bolshevik uprising.

Lenin's return to Russia after ten years of exile sparked the second phase of the Revolution. Lenin (center), in a beaver hat and dark coat, is flanked by his top lieutenant Leon Trotsky (wearing glasses) during a demonstration in Moscow's Red Square. Trotsky's closeness to Lenin earned him Stalin's eternal hatred.

The attack on the Winter Palace in Petrograd, where the provisional government was headquartered, began at dawn on November 7. By evening the Red Guard, Bolshevik soldiers led by Trotsky, had successfully taken most of the city. By the next morning, the Winter Palace had fallen with only six men killed.

And where was Stalin in this second and decisive phase of the Russian Revolution? According to his authorized biography published years later, he was by Lenin's side directing the fighting. Nothing could be further from the truth. While Trotsky was mobilizing the Red Guard to attack, Stalin was having tea with his old friends the Alliluyevs, whose daughter Nadezhda he planned to marry.

Within a week, Moscow fell to the Bolsheviks. In another week, all military installations were in their hands. The long road to revolution was at an end. Now Lenin would begin the difficult task of solidifying his power and turning Russia into a socialist state. The role Stalin would play in this new state was uncertain.

5

IN THE SHADOW OF LENIN

Stalin during the course of his
modest activity in the Executive
Committee gave one the impression,
and I was not alone in this view,
of a gray blur which flickered
obscurely and left no trace.
There is really nothing more to
be said about him.

Nikolay Sukhanov,
in *Notes on the*
Revolution, 1922[1]

Never refuse to do the little things,
because from the little things are
built the big. Stalin[2]

I N January 1918 a Constituent Assembly was elected
to form a new government in Moscow. It looked for a brief
moment as if Lenin might be willing to share power with
the other revolutionary groups. But when he saw that the
Bolsheviks were far outnumbered in the assembly, he had
the organization disbanded by the Red Guard. Russia's
first and only elected parliament lasted just one day.

Lenin's ultimate goal may have been a classless society where the state would, in Marx's words, "wither
away," but to arrive at that juncture the Bolshevik leader
was prepared to do whatever was necessary to retain
power. He created the Cheka, a secret police force that
would enforce the law, keep order, and intimidate and
attack anyone who didn't adhere to the party line. Similar
in spirit to the czar's Okharnka, the Cheka quickly proved
to be far more ruthless.

The Mensheviks and other groups who wanted a
more democratic government were incensed. Lenin further angered them by ending the war with Germany as he
had promised the Germans he would. The Treaty of Brest-
Litovsk was signed on March 3, 1918. Lenin paid a high
price for peace, giving up considerable territory to Germany, including the Baltic states, Poland, Georgia, and
the Ukraine.

One war ended, but another began almost at once—a
civil war between the Bolsheviks, now known as Communists (the Reds) and the anti-Communists (the Whites).
Like most civil wars, this one was brutal, with little mercy
shown by either side. The Whites should have had the
advantage, because there were many more of them, and
they had the support of such Western democracies as
France, Great Britain, and the United States. But, like the
provisional government that preceded them, the Whites

were poorly organized and had weak leadership. The Bolsheviks, under Lenin and Trotsky's direction, were a small but far more effective fighting force.

Earlier, Lenin had established a Politburo (Political Bureau) whose powers would supersede even those of the Central Committee. The first Politburo consisted of five members: Lenin, Trotsky, Stalin, Lev Kamenev, and Nikolai Bukharin, the brilliant theoretician of the party and editor of *Pravda*. Each man had his special area of interest—war, government, propaganda. Stalin was made commissar (minister) for nationalities. It was an impressive title, but gave him little power compared to the other commissars. He oversaw a small staff whose main function was to put out a weekly newspaper. Because he had less to do than the other commissars, Stalin began involving himself in their affairs, snatching a little power here and a little there. His meddling angered Trotsky, and Lenin had all he could do to keep the two from each other's throat. He appointed Stalin director of food supplies and sent him south with the Red Army to gather desperately needed grain and ship it north by train to Moscow and other cities. Stalin was delighted with the opportunity to show his leadership skills, and, as always, far exceeded the powers given him. He arrived in the city of Tsaritsyn on the Volga River and spent more time jailing and executing subversives and spies than overseeing the grain harvest. As commissar for war, Trotsky was supposed to deal with traitors, and he was furious with Stalin. At Trotsky's insistence, Stalin was recalled to Moscow. But he would not forget the city where he had his first taste of dictatorial power. Years later, Stalin would rename Tsaritsyn Stalingrad.

On March 24, 1919, Stalin married Nadezhda Alliluyeva. He was thirty-nine and she was only sixteen. But Nadezhda was neither sweet nor innocent like Stalin's first wife. She was a dedicated Communist, a child of the Revolution who worked directly under Lenin. As she grew older, Nadezhda would become a match for her dictatorial husband.

World War I had ended in 1918 with Germany's defeat, and the Allied Powers—including England and the United States—had withdrawn from Europe and stopped supporting the Whites in Russia. By the end of 1920, the civil war was all over. The Whites were completely crushed. Those who had not died in the fighting were sent to prison camps, exiled, or executed. The Bolsheviks had no one left to challenge their rule. In 1922 the Union of Soviet Socialist Republics (USSR) was born.

The Communist party ran the economy as well as the government. Private property had been abolished in 1918, but was brought back in 1921 to stimulate growth as part of the New Economic Policy. Only a tiny fraction of the population was allowed to join the Communist party, strengthening Lenin's rule by a small elite.

Stalin, who gained his position more for his dedication to hard work than his intellectual abilities, was given the job in the new government that no one else wanted—administration. As general secretary of the Central Committee, it was his duty to handle the day-to-day business of the Communist party. It was dull bureaucratic work. But Stalin was more than willing to take the burden of these petty details off the hands of his more lofty-minded colleagues.

Unlike Trotsky, who was always promoting himself in public, Stalin was content to remain in the shadow of Lenin, working away quietly in his Kremlin office. In the shadows he could go about the job of building his power base bit by bit, without attracting attention. In the shadows he could plot and conspire, and no one would know what he was up to—until it was too late.

As the new nation's top bureaucrat, Stalin had access to files on everyone in government. He quickly set about augmenting these files, building up a dossier on everyone in the party from Lenin on down. To accomplish this task, he created a "Special Section," a virtual spy network that kept reports on the personal lives of thousands of party officials. Houses were put under secret surveillance. Phone lines were bugged. Stalin's own wife served as a spy in Lenin's household, where she worked as his private secretary.

The people who worked for Stalin were treated well and promoted for good work. They owed their allegiance neither to Lenin nor to the state, but to Stalin. By the end of 1922, the country's chief filing clerk was nearly as powerful as Lenin himself, although few people realized it.

On the morning of May 26, 1922, a blood vessel burst in Lenin's brain, paralyzing the right side of his body. At age fifty-two, the leader of the Soviet Union was suddenly an invalid. Under doctors' orders, Lenin left Moscow and went to recuperate at his *dacha*, or country house, at Gorki, where Stalin was his most frequent visitor. The general secretary's concern for his leader was less than altruistic, though. Stalin was worried that Lenin had come to distrust him.

The general secretary had built up the government bureaucracy into a power unto itself. Lenin now saw that the people, the Revolution, the very cause of communism itself, were only a means to power for Stalin, whose motives became all the clearer to Lenin in their conversations at Gorki. Stalin wanted to concentrate all power in Moscow under the growing bureaucracy of the central government. Lenin felt this was dangerous and could lead to dictatorship. He wanted to share some of the state's power with the constituent republics, allowing them some say in how the country was run.

Stalin posed with his leader at Lenin's retreat in Gorki, where Lenin was recovering from his first stroke in 1922. The picture was released to the public shortly after Lenin's death and suggests an intimacy between the two men that, by this date, no longer existed.

If his health had been better, Lenin might have stopped Stalin. Instead, he bided his time, waiting for his strength to return. In the meantime, he had Trotsky to speak for him in the Central Committee. But Stalin was on his guard. He had Lenin's phone tapped and knew that he was conspiring with Trotsky against him.

Nine days before Christmas in 1922, Lenin suffered a second stroke. A week later, the partially paralyzed leader dictated a long letter addressed to his wife but really meant for the party leadership in Moscow. This historic document has come to be called Lenin's "Last Testament." In it, Lenin told how he wanted the government to be run after his death. He gave a penetrating critique of each member of the Politburo, reserving his harshest criticism for Stalin.

"Comrade Stalin," he wrote, "having become General Secretary, has concentrated unlimited power in his hands, and I am not sure whether he always knows how to use that power with sufficient caution. . . . Stalin is too rude, and this fault . . . [is] intolerable in the office of General Secretary. Therefore, I propose to the comrades to find a way to transfer Stalin from that position."3

If Lenin had published his testament in the early part of 1923, it might have all come to pass. But for some unexplained reason, Lenin put the document away in a drawer and waited. Perhaps he wanted to be well enough to read it himself before the Party Congress in April, where it would have the greatest effect. A few days before the Congress convened he suffered a third stroke that left him unable to move or speak.

Spring and summer came and went, and Lenin clung to life with stubborn tenacity. He began to speak again with difficulty, and there was real hope that he would yet recover his health. Back in Moscow, Stalin saw that time was running out. He couldn't attack Lenin, sick as he was, but he could go after Trotsky. Here, he found unexpected support from two powerful colleagues—Lev Kamenev and the party chief of Petrograd, Grigori Zinoviev. They were jealous of Trotsky's influence over the Red Army and feared he might make himself dictator after Lenin's death. Together with Stalin they formed a troika* to destroy Trotsky and seize control of the party for themselves. Kamenev and Zinoviev foolishly underestimated Stalin. They thought they could control him.

Together the three men spread rumors through the press that Trotsky was a man who could not be trusted. They brought up his Menshevik past and Jewish background to brand him as an outsider and a traitor to the state. Arrogant as always, Trotsky did little to defend himself, choosing to ignore the charges. While duck hunting with friends, Trotsky fell into icy water and developed a fever that the doctors could not diagnose. He left for a long rest in the Caucasus, leaving the troika to further undermine him.

Meanwhile, on January 21, 1924, Lenin suffered his fourth and final stroke. The father of Bolshevism was dead. The struggle between Stalin and Lenin was over, and Stalin had emerged victorious. Or had he? Lenin's "Last Testament" remained in his widow's possession, and she had every intention of reading it at the Party Congress in May to the assembled delegates. Stalin might well have guessed the bombshell the document contained, but there was little he could do to suppress it.

At long last, Joseph Stalin was ready to move out of the shadows and into the light of day. Would the burning light of truth destroy him as Lenin had intended?

* A troika is a Russian sled drawn by a team of three horses. It has come to mean any group of three people or nations acting together with equal power.

6 CLIMB TO POWER

*To choose one's victim, to pre-
pare one's plans minutely, to
slake on implacable vengeance,
and then to go to bed—there is
nothing sweeter in the world.*

Stalin to
Kamenev, 1923[1]

Stalin will strangle us all.

Bukharin to
Kamenev, 1928[2]

WHILE LENIN LIVED, Stalin was his worst enemy. Once Lenin was dead, Stalin became his most loyal follower. With dogged determination, he set out to turn the dead man into a demigod. Lenin's memory would live forever, his very corpse embalmed and encased in a mausoleum in the center of Moscow where all Russians could worship.

Lenin's widow was appalled. "To all these things he attached so little importance during life," she said.[3] Yet to Stalin they meant everything. Only by creating a cult around the dead leader could he legitimize himself as Lenin's heir. Appearance was everything. To the end of his days, this absolute dictator would humbly claim to be no more than "a follower of Lenin." The truth was that Lenin was Stalin's most valuable pawn in the deadly game of power he now played.

There was one person conspicuously absent at Lenin's funeral. Trotsky, weakened by illness, was en route from the Caucasus. Whether his failure to be at the ceremony was deliberately engineered by Stalin's giving him the wrong date for the funeral, or was an actual misunderstanding, the final result was the same. Trotsky's absence made him appear all the more cold and unfeeling to his peers.

But Stalin's own day of reckoning was fast approaching. Before the meeting of the 13th Soviet Congress, the Central Committee convened to hear Lenin's widow, Nadezhda Krupskaya, read her husband's "Last Testament." They would then decide if his words should be made known to the other delegates. Stalin sat stonily on the podium as Krupskaya read Lenin's condemnation of him. When she had finished, Grigori Zinoviev got up to speak:

Comrades, no one can doubt that every word of Ilyich [Lenin] is sacred to us. . . . But there is one point where, we are happy to say, Lenin's fears have proved groundless. I am speaking on the question of our General Secretary. All of you have witnessed our harmonious cooperation during these last months, and all of you, like me, have had the satisfaction of seeing that what Lenin feared has not taken place." 4

No one but Lenin's widow took issue with Zinoviev's statement. Why? It was not out of fear of Stalin that the Central Committee dismissed Lenin's charges against him. Stalin's allies needed his support in their fight to keep power from Trotsky. It never occurred to them that Stalin himself would become a far greater threat than Trotsky. The Committee's final decision was to read Lenin's Testament privately to only a few selected delegates to the Congress. Krupskaya was enraged and threatened to publish the document herself, but she never did. It would not be made public in the Soviet Union until 1956, three years after Stalin's death.

The 13th Congress was a mass of confusion. With Lenin gone, there was no clear vision for the future of the socialist state he had created. Trotsky, ever the radical, wanted to keep the Revolution alive by exporting communism to other countries, including Marx's homeland of Germany. The more conservative members of the Politburo, led by Bukharin, wanted to end the Revolution and create a strong Soviet Union before looking for new worlds to conquer. It was with these men that Stalin now sought to align himself.

Stalin's alliance with Kamenev and Zinoviev had outlived its usefulness. The man who had spoken up for

Stalin takes a winter stroll with three Kremlin allies, (left to right) Alexey Rykov, Kamenev, and Zinoviev. His alliance with the last two would soon fall apart when it no longer served his purpose.

Stalin, and saved him from disgrace and possible death, received no mercy from him now. Zinoviev was replaced as party leader in Leningrad (the new name for Petrograd) by Stalin's handpicked lieutenant, Sergei Kirov. When asked by a colleague if he knew what gratitude was, Stalin replied, "It is a sickness suffered by dogs."[5]

Expelled from the Politburo, Kamenev and Zinoviev moved quickly to form a new alliance with their old enemy Trotsky, who had been forced to resign as commissar of war in January 1925. But it was too late. Like frightened mice, they conspired in their hole against Stalin's hungry cat. The cat sat patiently, waiting for them to come out.

On the tenth anniversary of the Revolution, in November 1927, the Trotskyites upstaged Stalin's triumphant appearance at Lenin's tomb with a disruptive demonstration. Trotskyite leaflets were distributed from a papier-mâché dragon by Chinese students, part of Trotsky's International Communist movement. "Death to Stalin! Long live Trotsky!" they cried. There would never again be such open dissent against Stalin in Russia while he lived.

Two months later, Trotsky was arrested and led kicking and screaming from his home. He was exiled to Soviet Turkestan and expelled from the Soviet Union in 1929. Zinoviev and Kamenev were upbraided but allowed later to repent of their crimes. They were even invited back into the party—for a time.

With his old enemies out of the way, Stalin now turned on his new allies. He fell out with Bukharin over the issue of the peasants. Formerly, Stalin had agreed with him that the peasants should not be pushed to increase farm production until after the economy had stabilized. Now, he adopted Trotsky's policy of collectivizing Soviet agriculture and taking control of the farms away from the peasants. Bukharin, the one man who could have filled the leadership vacuum left by Lenin's death, now saw a bleak future in store for the Soviet Union. "The party is doomed," he despaired. "The state and the party have become one."[6] And both of these were in the hands of one man—Stalin.

With all his rivals vanquished, Stalin set about reconstructing the state in his own image. Lenin's New Economic Policy (NEP) had allowed some capitalism to exist in the country to ease the Soviet Union into socialism after the devastation of the civil war. Stalin ended this policy and eliminated all privately owned businesses. In 1928 he inaugurated the first of his five-year plans for economic development. Consumer goods, such as clothing and personal products, were neglected, and all efforts went into increasing the production of heavy industry to make the country strong and economically independent. But to increase production, workers had to be fed. The rapid increase of food production was vital.

In January 1928, Stalin paid his first and last visit to the farms of Siberia to check on the grain harvests. The most prosperous and able farmers, called *kulaks*, were reluctant to send their grain off to Moscow. One wily old kulak was not impressed by Stalin's position, nor by his request for grain. "Let me see you dance, young fellow," he said to the general secretary, "and then I will give you a bushel or two."[7]

Stalin was not amused. He would not forget the kulak's smug challenge. He would soon make the kulaks dance to his own tune—in a terrible dance of death.

7 GREAT STALIN

*Our breath, our blood, our life
here, take it, O Great Stalin!*

Alexis Tolstoy, writer[1]

*You are a tormentor, that's what
you are! You torment the whole
Russian people!*

Nadezhda Alliluyeva,
Stalin's wife[2]

ON DECEMBER 21, 1929, Joseph Stalin celebrated his fiftieth birthday. It was a momentous occasion. In the six years since Lenin's death, Stalin had crushed every rival. The "gray blur" had emerged as the unchallenged leader of the Soviet Union.

Now the time had come to transform Soviet society into a powerful nation worthy of a great leader. To increase productivity, Stalin decided that the 25 million private peasant farms that dotted the nation needed to be collectivized and taken over by the state, which would have access to the latest technology. Only by the collectivization of agriculture and the building of new industrial centers, Stalin firmly believed, could the Soviet Union catch up with the United States and the more advanced nations of Europe. "We are fifty to one hundred years behind the advanced countries," he said in a speech early in 1932. "We must catch up in ten years. Either we do it, or they crush us."[3]

The kulaks had the most to lose by collectivization and stubbornly resisted it. Stalin set about systematically eliminating them as a class.* Millions of kulaks were driven from their land. Some were executed, others forced into exile, and many more sent to labor camps where they were slowly worked to death. Their livestock and farm equipment were confiscated by the state and used on the new collective farms.

---

* Some historians question whether there were any kulaks left after the devastation of the civil war. A kulak by 1930 could have been any peasant who had a little more than his poorer neighbors—a cow, a few chickens, a small surplus of grain.

Many poor peasants were no more willing to give up their tiny patch of land to a collective farm than their betters. They rose up with pitchforks and axes and fought government troops sent to disarm them. Defeated by the troops, the desperate peasants destroyed everything they owned so that Stalin wouldn't get it. They slaughtered livestock and burned fields of crops. In a short time, they killed half the livestock and ruined half the produce in the Soviet Union. Stalin retaliated by forcing hundreds of thousands of them into exile. But many peasants who stayed behind faced an even crueler fate—starvation. Stalin took part in the devastation by withholding food supplies from rebellious peasants. The result was one of the worst artificially created famines in modern times.

Stalin had won in the battle of wills with the peasants. He had broken the back of the old Russia, and now he would begin to rebuild the new Soviet state in his own image. Millions of women and peasants were brought to new industrial cities in western Siberia, the Urals, and the Volga region and trained to be technicians, factory workers, and engineers. The Soviet economy began to grow and prosper.

The fact that more than 10 million people had died during this transformation mattered little to Stalin. He viewed people as his most expendable resource. There were always plenty more of them to take the place of the dead on the farms, in the factory lines, and in the ever-growing slave camps of Siberia.

While he transformed the country, Stalin was busy transforming himself from a practically unknown bureaucrat into his country's savior. To accomplish this feat, Stalin constructed one of the most incredible propaganda machines the world has ever seen.

The Stalin propaganda machine bombarded Soviets with pictures of their great leader once he achieved power. Here an artist shows the dictator sharing a happy moment with women delegates from Tadjikistan and Turkmenistan at a collective farmers' conference.

Stalin's idealized portrait—tall, handsome, his face unblemished—was hung in every public building and schoolroom. His name graced every map. Tsaritsyn was renamed Stalingrad (Stalin's City) as early as 1925. Towns, factories, streets, and buildings across Russia quickly followed suit. The hardest steel from Soviet mills was christened Stalinite. Poets and songwriters sang his praises. His glorious achievements were even immortalized in the Soviet national anthem. No title was too grandiose for the Soviet Union's supreme ruler. Father of the Peoples, Genius of Mankind, and Transformer of Nature were only a few.

Stalin wasn't content to transform himself in the present; he had to transform his past as well. He collaborated on his official biography, revising history to place himself in the center of every major event of the past twenty years. Those who said otherwise—be they friend or foe—were jailed, exiled, or executed.

Stalin re-created himself out of feelings of inferiority, fear, and political expediency. Through his unceasing campaign of propaganda he became a mythic figure of almost supernatural proportions. The words "Thanks be to Stalin!" replaced "Thanks be to God!" whenever something good happened in a person's life.

Other gods had no place in Stalin's Soviet Union. The former choirboy from Gori set out to systematically destroy organized religion, especially the age-old Russian Orthodox Church. The Bolsheviks had begun a campaign against religion long before Stalin came to power, but Stalin accelerated the process with a savage enthusiasm all his own. He banned not only church services but religious books and other printed materials. Churches across the country were turned into clubs and movie theaters. The largest and most famous churches were either torn down or became museums to atheism. While many Russians stubbornly clung to their beliefs despite these draconian measures, half of the population had turned its back on religion by the mid-1930s.

While religion was condemned, the arts were allowed to flourish, but only to serve the state. Modern movements in literature, art, and music, such as surrealism, expressionism, and naturalism, were openly condemned as decadent. Soviet artists were encouraged to pursue a new Stalinist style of creative expression called "socialist realism." Socialist realism was, contrary to its name, anything but reality. It depicted peasants as happy and well fed, revolutionaries as brave and fearless, and workers as satisfied and well treated. It was a fairy-tale picture of a perfect society with no problems or injustices. As Stalin's regime continued, such images became more and more removed from reality.

For all this, Stalin seems to have had a soft spot in his steely heart for true artists, whom he called "engineers of the soul." The contrary nature of Russia's number one patron of the arts can be glimpsed in his relationships with three Soviet creative geniuses.

Maksim Gorky was the most celebrated author of revolutionary Russia. Although he enthusiastically supported the Bolsheviks, Gorky chose to leave his homeland during the civil war and lived in Italy until 1928. That year Stalin invited him back to Russia to celebrate the author's sixtieth birthday. Gorky accepted the invitation and crossed the country as a goodwill ambassador for the "new Russia." But much of what Gorky saw—Stalin's repression, censorship, and authoritarianism—disturbed him. He soon became the spokesman for dissenting artists and writers, earnestly trying to get Stalin to work toward what Gorky called a "kinder, gentler" government. Stalin tolerated Gorky as long as he could use him and his reputation to further his own ends. The writer died suddenly on June 18, 1936, of a mysterious illness. A few years later Stalin announced that Gorky had been poisoned by his doctors in collaboration with Stalin's own chief of police. If this is true, and there is no direct evidence to prove it, it was surely at Stalin's order.

Stalin's taste in literature was remarkably good, but his taste in music was far more rudimentary. He loved the simple folk music of his native Georgia, but classical music largely bored him. For all that, Stalin set himself up as his nation's most powerful music critic. Every record made in the Soviet Union was sent to him before its release, and he'd dutifully listen to it on his phonograph. Each record received one of four ratings: good, so-so, bad, or rubbish. One of his favorite recordings was of a woman singer backed by a chorus of barking dogs.

In the 1920s, Dmitry Shostakovich emerged as the boy wonder of serious Russian music. In the 1930s, Shostakovich turned to writing opera. His *Lady Macbeth of the Mtsensk District* was a harshly realistic retelling of Shakespeare's tragedy *Macbeth* set in Soviet Russia. It was an artistic and popular success and ran in one theater for two years.

One night in January 1936, Stalin attended a performance and hated it. This was not uplifting music for the masses. The opera closed at once. An article in *Pravda* appeared under the headline, "Muddle Instead of Music." Unless the composer reformed his ways, the writer darkly threatened, he "could end very badly." Shostakovich got the message and returned to writing symphonic music with a definite patriotic theme. He never wrote another opera.

If Stalin had a favorite among the arts it was the cinema. He indulged his passion for movies by screening as many as two or three in one evening for his friends and guests. American movies were his favorites, especially the Tarzan films, of which he was proud owner of a complete collection.

Sergei Eisenstein is today considered the greatest of all the Russian filmmakers. His silent films *The Battleship Potemkin* and *Ten Days That Shook the World,* with their brilliant use of lightning-fast editing, are masterpieces.

In 1940, Eisenstein started work on an epic three-part film of the life of Ivan IV, better known as Ivan the Terrible, the czar who unified Russia in the sixteenth century. Ivan was a tyrant on a scale that only Stalin could appreciate. His paranoiac personality led Ivan to see enemies, both real and imagined, all around him. Stalin took great interest in the project and was so impressed by the first part of *Ivan the Terrible* that he awarded Eisenstein the Stalin Prize for it. He was less enthusiastic about the second part, which he saw at a private screening in 1946.

Soon after, Stalin met with the director and celebrated Russian actor Nikolay Cherkasov, who played Ivan in the films. Here is Cherkasov's account of their meeting:

> *While referring to Ivan the Terrible's mistakes, [Stalin] remarked that they partly consisted of a failure to fight the feudal lords to the end. Had he done this, Russia would have had no Time of Troubles. At this point [he] added humorously, "There God stood in Ivan's way." Ivan the Terrible would liquidate one feudal family, one boyar clan,* and would then repent for a whole year and pray for forgiveness of his "sins" when instead he should have been acting with increasing determination.*4

Stalin might have been thinking about his own brand of "increasing determination," which he had used effectively to exterminate the kulaks fifteen years before.

Most Soviet artists, like the rest of the population, looked on their leader as little less than a demigod. But there was one person who saw Stalin in far more human terms and wasn't afraid to stand up to him—his wife Nadezhda Alliluyeva. A totally committed Communist, she had believed her husband was one of the new men of the Soviet state. After the war with the peasants, she came to the sad realization that Stalin was just another tyrant in a long line of Russian tyrants, a czar to rival Ivan the Terrible himself. The couple's relationship deteriorated. Stalin was unfaithful to Nadezhda and spoke rudely to her in public. She responded by accusing him of infidelity and murder.

---

* The boyars were the old nobility of Russia. Ivan virtually wiped them out to consolidate his power as czar.

On November 7, 1932, the fifteenth anniversary of the Revolution, Stalin talked coarsely to his wife during a gala dinner party, ordering her to have a drink. She left the party in a fury. What happened next is shrouded in mystery. In his memoirs, Stalin's successor, Nikita Khrushchev, claimed that Nadezhda waited for Stalin at home and started calling his friends to find out where he was. A loose-tongued duty officer told her that her husband was with the wife of a high-ranking military officer. Whether it was out of raging jealousy or self-disgust over her life with Russia's butcher, Nadezhda is reported to have shot herself during the night with a tiny Walther pistol, a gift from a relative. Some people question this official account to this day. Some of those present in the house at the time claim that Stalin arrived home, had a violent argument with Nadezhda, and that she died in a struggle over the pistol.

We may never know what really happened that night, but Nadezhda's death, at age thirty, deeply wounded Stalin. According to their daughter Svetlana, who adheres to the suicide theory, Nadezhda left a letter for Stalin accusing him of monstrous crimes. He did not attend her funeral and didn't visit her grave for years. In Stalin's paranoiac mind, his wife had betrayed him. If she could do so, he thought, so could anyone. This belief would have murderous consequences in the dark years ahead.

8 REIGN OF TERROR

Life is better comrades,
life is gayer.

Stalin in a speech
at the Congress
of Victors, 1934[1]

The enemies of Stalin are
the enemies of Russia.
The Special Division is to
ensure that no enemies
of Stalin continue to live.

Genrikh Yagoda,
head of the
NKVD [police][2]

THE TERM "REIGN OF TERROR" originated in revolutionary France in 1793. The radical Jacobin leaders instituted a policy of terror in order to destroy their enemies, impose order, and create a democratic state. What followed was the arrest, trial, and execution of tens of thousands of French citizens, many of them guilty of no crime. There have been other institutionalized terrors before and since the Jacobins, but the one begun by Stalin in the Soviet Union in the mid-1930s differs in one important way from all the others.

In revolutionary France and elsewhere a policy of terror was a response to a real threat to the government in power, however excessive that reaction might have been. In Stalin's Soviet Union, no such threat existed. By 1934, Stalin was in complete control of his country. Many people may have hated him, but they were powerless and unable to harm him. He had no reason to persecute his countrymen. The millions who died in those nightmare years of 1936 to 1938 were innocent of any crime against their country or Stalin.

Why did it happen? To find the answer we have to look to Stalin's character. For all his power, Stalin was a man consumed by fear. Death and pain terrified him. He never flew in an airplane, avoided the dentist (he'd rather let his teeth rot than undergo drilling), and traveled everywhere in a sealed, bulletproof train or a car with a machine gun under the seat. Stalin's fear of assassination was truly pathological. Even his most trusted aides were frisked regularly by guards before entering his presence.

Despite these strict precautions Stalin still didn't feel safe. He knew it was brute force that kept him in power and that there were many people, both in and out of government, who hated and feared him. Despite his bluff front, he was well aware that some of his policies had failed. While the economy was growing, the first five-year plan had fallen far short of Stalin's high goals, and statistics were falsified to convince the people otherwise.

Stalin believed the old guard of Bolsheviks still looked on him as the upstart Georgian with the withered arm and thick accent, and he hated them for it. This hatred extended to anyone who had known him before he became Great Stalin. They knew about his deviousness, his years of obscurity as a revolutionary, his cowardice, and possibly his employment as an informant for the czar's police. Stalin could not rest until these people were all eliminated, purged from his presence and his memory.

However, he was in no hurry to spring the trap. He wanted his "enemies" to feel relaxed and safe. The 17th Party Congress of January 1934, known as the Congress of Victors, was a harmonious celebration of the new Soviet state. Kamenev and Bukharin and other leaders who had fallen from favor admitted their mistakes and were welcomed back into the party with open arms. Stalin seemed conciliatory, good-humored, and reassuring. (Of those delegates who applauded his speeches and laughed with him, half would not be alive to attend the next Congress.) All the while, Stalin was on the lookout for some justification to begin his purge, some hard evidence of a conspiracy against him.

Stalin's reign of terror began with the murder of one man. If anyone was capable of replacing Stalin in 1934, it was Sergei Kirov, the immensely popular party boss of Leningrad. Like Russian leader Boris Yeltsin in the 1990s, Kirov was a charismatic man of the people. He liked nothing better than to enter a crowd and press the flesh, something Stalin would never have dreamed of doing. Others in the Kremlin may have seen Kirov as a successor to Stalin, but not Kirov himself. When rumors of such a plan reached him, he dutifully told Stalin all about it. "Thank you, Comrade Kirov," was Stalin's only reply. Although he didn't know it, Kirov had signed his own death warrant.

On December 1, 1934, at 4:30 P.M., Leonid Nikolayev, a disgruntled former civil servant, fatally shot Kirov in the hall outside his office at party headquarters in Leningrad. The assassination was portrayed as part of a vast conspiracy directed from abroad by Trotsky. In fact, the assassin had been handpicked for the job by Genrikh Yagoda, the head of the People's Commissariat of Internal Affairs, Stalin's secret police, better known as the NKVD. The assassination had been carefully worked out to the second. Earlier that day, Nikolayev had been stopped by guards at party headquarters with a gun found on him. He was released a short time later, before the shooting, under NKVD orders and his gun was returned to him.

Stalin was publicly distraught at the death of the man he had ordered killed. He arranged a spectacular funeral for Kirov and renamed the Soviet Union's leading dance company after him—the Kirov Ballet. Slowly he began setting up the machinery for the terror. On the day of Kirov's death, a law was passed that allowed an accused person to be tried by an appointed court without a decent defense and with no hope of appeal.

Then, in August 1936, the ax fell. A small group of Bolshevik leaders, led by Kamenev and Zinoviev, went on public trial for treason in Moscow. This was the first of three so-called show trials, centerpieces of the great purge. The word "show" is fitting because this was a form of public theater, meant to show the world that these men were guilty of unspeakable crimes. Nothing was left to chance. Each day's testimony was carefully scripted and even rehearsed in advance by accusers and accused. Each of the accused confessed his sins against the state in

Stalin (center) follows the coffin of his friend and protégé Sergei Kirov in the solemn funeral procession for the slain party boss of Leningrad. Kirov's death in 1934 was the excuse Stalin needed to begin a reign of terror that would take the lives of 6 to 8 million Russians.

elaborate detail, explaining his part in a plot of truly Byzantine intrigue. Because they confessed so readily, no further proof of their guilt was necessary for conviction.

Why did these men go to their deaths so willingly, without the least resistance? Stalin had made sure that by the time they appeared in the courtroom all the fight had been knocked out of them. Due to the public nature of the trials, physical torture that could have left marks was out of the question. Instead, the accused were subjected to months of psychological torture that included round-the-clock interrogation, bright lights in their cells, and sleep deprivation. If all else failed, the men were told that unless they confessed, their entire families would be killed. Under this threat even the strongest of them caved in.

The show trial's climax was the final confession of the accused before sentencing. Here is Kamenev's last speech in court:

> *I have stained my sons' names. I want them to know my last wish, which is that they should work, fight, and if be die only under the banner of Stalin. If I have failed to serve my socialist fatherland in life, then let this service be rendered by my death.*[3]

Stalin was ready to oblige. Kamenev, Zinoviev, and all the other defendants were condemned and summarily executed. Their deaths had none of the public grandeur of the guillotine nor the dignity of a firing squad. One by one, they were taken at night to a basement cell in the infamous headquarters of the NKVD on Lubyanka Street and shot in the head. The grim ritual was described unemotionally by an NKVD officer who later defected:

> *Before execution the prisoner changes into white underclothes only. He knows that he has been sentenced and is about to be executed. He is led into the death cell, where he is shot in the back of the head by the executioner, either as he stands facing the wall or just as he walks into the cell. . . . A tarpaulin is spread on the floor of the cell, and a woman is employed to clean up afterwards. The bodies are taken away and buried immediately in a common grave.*[4]

As the second show trial began in 1937, the scenario grew more strange and surreal. Unhappy with Yagoda's performance in carrying out his duty, Stalin had him replaced by Nikolai Yezhov, a short, ruthless man, whose bloodthirstiness rivaled his master's. (His nickname was "The Bloody Dwarf.") Yezhov intensified the terror with methodical thoroughness. Hundreds of lower party officials were arrested as part of the mysterious Trotskyite conspiracy and put on trial. Two or three times a week Yezhov would send Stalin a neatly typed list of victims for his approval. Stalin would skim the death list and carelessly initial it. Soon to appear on the list was Yagoda himself, who under torture confessed to Kirov's murder. Along with him died the three thousand men in the NKVD who carried out his orders.

Guilt by association became a familiar pattern as the terror accelerated. A low-ranking party official would be accused of a crime and forced through torture to implicate his boss. Step by step, up the ladder of the party hierarchy, the accusations would continue until half the government was accused of treason. Then each of the accused's family, friends, and acquaintances would be arrested, tried, and executed or sent to a labor camp. Stalin wanted no survivors left to seek revenge.

The reaction of the Soviet people to this exposed network of conspiracy was one of complete shock. The idea that all these dedicated men who had helped build the Communist state were traitors was almost inconceivable. But such was the grip of Stalin's authority that many did believe it, while others simply said nothing, fearing they would be swept up by the terror themselves. As writer Isaac Babel put it, "Today a man only talks freely with his wife—at night, with the blankets pulled over his head."[5]

Foreign observers were invited to sit in on the show trials. Although most of them remained deeply suspicious, American ambassador to Russia Joseph E. Davies came to the second show trial a skeptic and left a true believer.

"The purge . . . cleared the country and rid it of treason," he later wrote in his best-selling book *Mission to Moscow*.[6] He concluded that the trials couldn't have been rigged because it "would have taken the creative genius of a Shakespeare to stage them!"[7]

If Davies had attended the third show trial, his faith in Stalin might have been shaken, for one of the participants had the colossal nerve to depart from the prepared script. The man was Bukharin, who, knowing he would die anyway, refused to play the penitent sinner in Stalin's play. Bukharin fully admitted there was a "monstrous conspiracy" afoot. "The conspirators are Stalin and Yezhov," he proclaimed. "Stalin wants to establish his absolute power over the party and the state, and to reach this position it is necessary for him to ride roughshod over all obstacles. That is why we are to be eliminated."[8] Bukharin's boldness was refreshing, but it did not save him from the cellars.

Next, Stalin turned his murderous gaze toward the military. His first target was a hero of the Revolution and the civil war—Marshal Tukhachevsky. The general was accused of being a spy in the pay of Nazi Germany and Japan. Tukhachevsky was tried, convicted, and executed, along with seven other leading generals. But this was only the beginning. Before he was through, Stalin had 35,000 officers executed, half of the entire corps.

And still the terror continued to spread. In its ultimate phase the ordinary citizen, who until now had been a mere observer of the horror, became its victim. Informers were encouraged to turn on their neighbors, friends, and family members for a reward of one fourth of the victim's property. Obtaining confessions took far less time in the case of the average person because physical torture could be applied. Since there would be no public trial, no one would see the marks and scars.

The terror was running so smoothly by now that many of these victims had no idea that Stalin was their chief persecutor. They blamed their misfortune on Yezhov or other underlings, often going to their deaths praising Stalin. "If only Stalin knew!" was the common cry heard from victims and their families.

No one was safe, even those closest to Stalin. A misinterpreted comment, a lingering stare could be a man's doom. Nikita Khrushchev recalled his own close call at a meeting with Stalin in the Kremlin:

His face was, as usual, absolutely expressionless. He looked at me and said, "You know, Antipov has been arrested." Nikolai Antipov was a prominent politician from Leningrad.

"No, I didn't know," I answered.

"Well," said Stalin, "he had some evidence against you." He was staring into my eyes with that blank look of his.

I stared back, at first not knowing what to say. Then I answered, "I don't know anything about the whole business. But I do know that Antipov could not offer any evidence against me, because we've had only a nodding acquaintance."

I think Stalin was trying to read something in my eyes. Whatever he saw there gave him no reason to suspect any link between me and Antipov. If he'd somehow got the impression that I was trying to hide something, well, the world might soon have learned about a new enemy of the people.[9]

During these nightmarish years, Stalin's home life stood in sharp contrast to the horror going on around him. He had three children—Svetlana and Vasily from his second marriage, and Yakov from his first. Stalin cared little for his two sons, both of whom disappointed him. Vasily was a lazy ne'er-do-well who would later turn to drink as his grandfather had. Yakov was a gentle soul, like his mother, who cared nothing about personal ambition and wanted a quiet life. Stalin hated his elder son for his sensitivity and would mock him before his friends. When Yakov attempted to shoot himself and failed, Stalin's only recorded remark was, "He couldn't even do that right!"

What fatherly affection Stalin had he lavished on his daughter. "He spoiled me and loved playing games with me," Svetlana wrote years later. "I was his rest and relaxation." He called her "Housekeeper" and referred to himself as her "wretched Secretary." His letters to her show a side of Stalin rarely glimpsed elsewhere. Here is a sample from April 1935:

> I'm sending you pomegranates, tangerines and some candied fruit. Eat and enjoy them my little Housekeeper! I'm not sending any to Vasya [Vasily] because he's still doing badly at school and feeds me nothing but promises. . . .
> I report to you, Comrade Housekeeper, that I was in Tiflis [Tbilisi] for one day. I was at my mother's and I gave her regards from you and Vasya. She is well, more or less, and she gives both of you a big kiss. Well, that's all right now. I give you a kiss. I'll see you soon.
>
> From Setanka—Housekeeper's wretched Secretary, the poor peasant J. Stalin[10]

In the winter of 1938, the terror ended as quietly as it had begun. Among the last victims was Stalin's head execu-

Stalin is seen in a rare affectionate mood with his daughter Svetlana around 1936. His warmth toward her cooled as she grew older. By the end of World War II, most of the members of Stalin's family would be killed or in prison under his orders.

tioner, Yezhov. Stalin felt Yezhov was getting too ambitious and would soon want his job. He replaced him with Lavrenty P. Beria, a neatly dressed, bespectacled bureaucrat and a fellow Georgian. Beria was every bit as ambitious as his predecessor but was a far smoother politician. He would make himself indispensable to Stalin and remain in power until Stalin's death fifteen years later.

Stalin's reign of terror claimed between seven and nine million victims. At least a million of these were executed. Most of the rest died a slow, lingering death in Stalin's gulag, a chain of labor camps that stretched across the Soviet Union. Stalin used prisoners like firewood to stoke the furnace of the camps. Prisoners worked until they died of beatings, illness, or exhaustion. A few years later, Hitler would pattern his concentration camps after this grisly Soviet model.

By the end of 1938 there were only a few survivors of the first generation of Bolshevik revolutionaries, the most prominent being Stalin and Trotsky. Trotsky had served a useful purpose during the purges as a scapegoat for the imagined conspiracy against Stalin. In truth, he was now a harmless old man with few supporters, moving from country to country and writing his books. But the time had come, Stalin decided, for him to join the others. Since 1936, Trotsky had been living in a villa just outside Mexico City. Several NKVD attempts on Trotsky's life had failed, thanks to the vigilance of his bodyguards.

On August 20, 1940, Trotsky was visited at home by a young friend and supporter, Ramón Mercader. As the old revolutionary sat at his desk writing, Mercader, an undercover NKVD agent, took a pickax from under his coat and smashed Trotsky's skull. He died the next day. The book he had been working on at the moment of his death was a biography of Joseph Stalin.

9

THE FORTUNES OF WAR

In both Stalinism and fascism we see an insatiable thirst for power, a yearning to remake the world according to a particular design, and the same contempt for human beings.

A. Varara, in a
Minsk newspaper[1]

Stalin must command our unconditional respect. In his own way he is a hell of a fellow. Stalin is half beast, half giant.

Adolf Hitler, 1942[2]

WHILE STALIN was purging his country of millions of potential enemies, another dictator was solidifying his power in nearby Germany—Adolf Hitler.

Hitler, like Stalin, was a man consumed by ambition and hate. A failed Austrian artist, Hitler became a leader of the German National Socialist party, better known as the Nazi party, founded in Munich, Germany, in 1920. Although they used the word "Socialist," the Nazis were fascists who yearned to raise Germany from the ashes of defeat after World War I and transform it into the most powerful nation in Europe. After years of setbacks, Hitler became chancellor of Germany in 1933. In just a few years, he revived German industry and built his country into a powerful military state. By 1939 he was ready to embark on a war of conquest.

Like other heads of state, Stalin saw the war coming and knew the Soviet Union was in no shape to fight Germany. His purging of the Red Army had left the largest army in Europe leaderless.* The Russian people were demoralized and exhausted by the terror, and the economy was faltering. More than anything, Stalin wanted to appease Hitler. Thus the man who had murdered millions of his own people who meant him no harm struck up a friendship with a man who would become his mortal enemy. It was an error in judgment for which Stalin—and Russia—would pay dearly.

Although ideological opposites on the surface, Stalin and Hitler had much in common. Both were tyrants who had ambitions of world domination. It was this lust for

---

* It is estimated that during the terror, Stalin killed more of his own officers than Hitler did during all of World War II.

power that finally brought them together in the summer of 1939.

Hitler had designs on Poland, the nation that geographically separated him from the Soviet Union. However, he wanted assurances that Stalin wouldn't come to Poland's defense if he attacked. Stalin, on his part, wanted Hitler's assurance that he wouldn't keep marching through Poland and invade the Soviet Union. Stalin also coveted eastern Poland for himself.

On August 23, 1939, Germany and the Soviet Union signed a nonaggression pact, vowing not to go to war against one another and agreeing to divide Poland between them. On hearing of the treaty's signing in Moscow, Hitler is reported to have jumped for joy, shouting, "I have the world in my pocket!"[3] Having neutralized the Soviets, he could now go to war against the rest of Europe.

A little more than a week later, the Germans marched on Poland. Two days later France and Great Britain declared war on Germany. Two weeks later Stalin invaded eastern Poland. The West, which would not know the full details of the "Pact of Blood" with Germany until the war's end, was shocked by Stalin's aggression. So were many faithful Communists in the Soviet Union and abroad who couldn't believe that Stalin would befriend the hated Nazis.

As Hitler lay siege to the Netherlands, Belgium, and Luxembourg, Stalin moved forward to take over the Baltic states of Estonia, Latvia, and Lithuania, as well as parts of Romania. Then he made his second major blunder and attacked his neighbor to the northwest, Finland. Stalin felt he needed Finland as a buffer against any attack from the West. When the Finns refused to sell him part of their territory, he declared war on them. Stalin predicted he would take Finland in three weeks. Instead, it took him three long, agonizing months.

Soviet Foreign Minister Molotov signs the infamous "Pact of Blood" between his country and Nazi Germany in August 1939 under Stalin's approving gaze. Stalin hoped the non-aggression treaty would protect him from Hitler's war machine, but the Nazis invaded Russia less than two years later after subduing most of the rest of Europe.

Finland was a small but fiercely independent country that had been under the yoke of czarist Russia and didn't intend to be enslaved again. Dressed in white to blend into the wintry landscape, the Finnish soldiers swooped down on skis, attacking the invaders like angels of death. They invented a new weapon to use against the enemy—the "Molotov cocktail." Named after the Soviet minister who signed the Pact of Blood with Germany, it was a deadly concoction of kerosene, tar, and gasoline, put into a whiskey bottle with a piece of rag wrapped around it. Saboteurs hurled the cocktails into Russian tanks, where they exploded, turning the tanks into fiery infernos.

The Soviets won the "Winter War" against Finland, but at a terrible price. The defeated Finns lost 25,000 men, the Soviets, almost ten times as many. The Winter War exposed Stalin's vulnerability to the world at a time when he could least afford it.

Meanwhile, Hitler's war machine was steamrolling across western Europe with frightening speed. Denmark, Norway, Holland, Belgium, Luxembourg, and finally France collapsed in quick succession like a row of dominoes. By the spring of 1940, Hitler was ready to launch an air assault on Europe's last bastion of democracy, Britain. Britain's courageous prime minister, Winston Churchill, led his countrymen in a valiant resistance to Hitler's attack. After months of bombing raids did little to break Britain, Hitler temporarily halted the assault on London in October 1940 and turned his guns east to his old ally, the Soviet Union. He had intended from the start to conquer the Soviet Union and use its vast natural resources and people to help complete his world conquest. The nonaggression pact with Stalin had merely been a stalling technique.

Stalin should have expected no better at Hitler's hands. But incredibly, as Hitler massed his forces at the

This grimly comic editorial cartoon appeared in U.S. newspapers after Stalin's surprise invasion of Finland. The caption reads "Next." At least four of the waiting countries would feel the sharp blade of the Soviet sickle, but only after Stalin himself had received the closest of shaves from Hitler.

Soviet border, Stalin continued to put his faith in the German leader. He received warnings of the Nazis' intentions months before the attack—from the British, from his own spies, and even from a German deserter who gave him the exact time of the invasion. But Stalin refused to believe any of them. Like a man with a terminal disease, he refused to listen to the doctor's diagnosis and clung to the illusion that nothing was wrong. At dawn on Sunday, June 22, 1941, illusion gave way to reality.

Hitler had chosen the date for his attack carefully. It was the anniversary of Napoleon's invasion of Russia 129 years earlier. Three and a half million soldiers marched across the border meeting little or no resistance from the unprepared Russians. At the most critical moment of his career, the man of steel turned to jelly. Too stunned to give the order for his soldiers to defend themselves, Stalin locked himself in a room of his dacha and drank himself into a stupor. He wasn't seen or heard from for four days. In two weeks, German troops were 300 miles (480 kilometers) inside the Soviet Union. Hitler was confident he would take Moscow in six more weeks.

Stalin's horror at the invasion was only surpassed by the realization that many of his people welcomed it. Under Stalin, Russia had become a vast prison for millions, and many of them embraced the Nazis as liberators. Only when the Nazis treated them with the same brutality as their leader, did they give their allegiance back to Stalin, preferring the devil they knew to a new one.*

Meanwhile, the Germans continued their relentless march toward Moscow, averaging 20 miles (32 kilometers) a day. Hitler also sent troops north to take Leningrad and south to invade the Ukraine and cut off the country from its main source of food supplies, Ukrainian grain. By early July, Stalin finally came to his senses. But the Soviet defense was so disorganized that there was little he could do immediately to hold back the Germans.

If Hitler had continued to push forward, the history of World War II might have been very different. But overconfidence got the better of him, and he made his first grave mistake. Two hundred miles (320 kilometers) from Moscow he called off the advance and deployed more troops to Leningrad and the Ukraine. By the time the march on Moscow resumed in September, Stalin was better prepared to fight. His strongest ally was an unusually bitter Russian winter.

Although he gave himself the title of generalissimo, Stalin was not a great wartime leader. He had no grasp of

* Despite the Nazis' cruelty, 400,000 Soviets fought on the German side.

elementary military strategy and wasted men and resources on a staggering scale. He stunned his own generals by drawing his operational lines on a 10-foot-diameter (3-meter) globe because he was too lazy to bother with far more accurate military maps.

Where Stalin did excel, however, was in the political theater of war propaganda. The leader of the Communist world suddenly conjured up the glorious czarist past in speech after speech, urging the Soviet people to imitate such historical figures as Alexander Nevsky, who defended Russia from the invading Teutonic tribes in the thirteenth century. Stalin even enlisted the support of the Russian Orthodox Church in the war effort, by allowing a religious revival in the Soviet Union. The people rallied to the defense of "Mother Russia," temporarily forgetting Stalin's former destruction of organized religion.

Perhaps Stalin's wisest decision was to remain in Moscow while the rest of the government fled the capital in the bleak days of October. With the Nazis only 40 miles (64 kilometers) away, people were burning their party membership cards, so they couldn't be identified as Communists. But Stalin held firm. This one uncharacteristic act of courage went a long way toward making Stalin more beloved to the Soviet people than anything else he had done in fifteen years of power.

The courage of the Soviet people and the frigid cold of one of the worst winters on record worked together to repel the Germans and save Moscow. But Hitler had only begun to fight. He continued his siege of Leningrad and then set his sights on the city especially dear to Stalin, Stalingrad. Stalingrad would be the setting for the showdown between Europe's two mightiest tyrants. For seven long months the Germans laid siege to Stalingrad. Stalin was fortunate to finally find a general who could match the abilities of the top generals he had killed in the purges, Marshal Georgy Zhukov. Zhukov's plan was to encircle the invading Nazis with one million soldiers. Helped by another freezing Russian winter, the Soviet troops eventually beat the Germans into submission.

By February 1943, 91,000 German soldiers surrendered to the Soviets. The battle for Stalingrad ended in a decisive victory for Stalin and a crushing defeat for Hitler. For the first time, the world saw that the Nazi war machine was not invincible. Soon the Germans were retreating from Russian soil, giving up the land they had won bit by bit. It was the beginning of the end for Hitler.

Zhukov may have won the victory but, as usual, Stalin took most of the credit. While propaganda posters showed Stalin visiting the front lines and encouraging battle-weary soldiers, there is little evidence that he ever ventured anywhere near the front or talked to a single soldier. He spent most of the war out of sight, safely ensconced behind his desk in his Kremlin office, only a few steps from a private elevator that would take him to a bomb shelter 155 (32 meters) feet below ground.

Stalin's troops had no such security. The common Soviet soldier led a miserable existence, worse than those of any other warring nation at the time. They were poorly clothed and armed, received scant medical care, and were given no home leave. Special units of the NKVD watched soldiers closely, and anyone who ran from battle or broke a military regulation was severely punished. "In the Red Army it takes more courage to retreat than to advance," Stalin said with grim humor.4

The cruelest fate of all was reserved for prisoners of war. There was no word for surrender in Stalin's vocabulary. A Soviet soldier was expected to fight to the death. If captured, it was a soldier's duty to kill himself on the spot;

to be taken alive was tantamount to treason. Even those closest to Stalin could expect no mercy. His elder son, Yakov, a Soviet artillery lieutenant, was captured by the Germans. The Nazis offered to exchange him for a captured German general. Stalin refused, stating coldly, "I have no son called Yakov."5 Stalin's son spent four years in a German prison camp before dying. Some say he was shot trying to escape. Other sources claim he flung himself on a barbed wire fence and begged to be shot.

Those Soviet prisoners who did eventually return home after the war came to regret their decision. They were a double threat to Stalin. First, they had had the effrontery to survive and were branded traitors. Second, they had seen life outside the Soviet Union and might never again be content with life under Stalin's austere regime. Such men could never be trusted and would only contaminate the general population, Stalin reasoned. So these soldiers who had suffered so much for their homeland were shot or sent to a lingering death in a labor camp. The only Soviet war hero, in Stalin's eyes, was a dead one or one lucky enough to escape capture.

After the Japanese attacked Pearl Harbor on December 7, 1941, the United States entered the war. The American and British Allied forces suddenly found themselves on the same side as the Russians, fighting a common enemy, the Axis powers of Germany, Japan, and Italy. The Soviet Union's courageous stand against the invading Germans captured the hearts and imaginations of the Allies. Stalin's previous crimes against his own people were conveniently forgotten, and he was now perceived as kindly, white-mustached "Uncle Joe" in a military greatcoat with a pipe firmly clenched between his teeth.

This image served Stalin well when the Big Three— U.S. president Franklin Roosevelt, Churchill, and

The "Big Three" met for the first time in Teheran, Iran, in 1943 to plan strategy in their war against Hitler. Although Franklin Roosevelt (center) and Winston Churchill (right), both skillful politicians, appear to be pleased with Stalin, in fact, the alliance was shaky from the start.

Stalin—met together in Teheran, Iran, in November 1943 to plan their strategy against Hitler. Roosevelt, who had never met Stalin before, knew little about him. He thought he could handle Stalin merely by humoring him. Churchill, who had dealt enough with Stalin to know better, was wary of the Soviet leader. Roosevelt even made jokes at his British ally's expense to show Stalin his good intentions.

Stalin promised to give full support to the planned Allied invasion of France the following June by mounting a massive assault on Germany from the east. In his heart of hearts, however, Stalin hoped to make France and the rest of Western Europe his own after driving out the Germans.

The D-Day landing of the Allied forces at Normandy, France, on June 6, 1944, was the largest land invasion in history. While the Germans were being driven from France, Stalin was attacking them on the eastern front in Hungary and Romania. In Poland, Stalin showed his true colors. Soviet propaganda encouraged the Poles in the city of Warsaw to revolt against their German masters. It was a heroic but doomed struggle. Soviet soldiers watched and waited just outside Warsaw as the Nazis slaughtered its citizens. They saved Stalin the trouble of subduing the Poles himself. Not until the killing was over did the Soviets march in and take the city. Warsaw's so-called liberation by the Soviets was countered by the freeing of Nazi-occupied Paris by the Allies on August 24, 1944.

As the Nazis retreated into Germany for the final phase of the war, the Soviets advanced on them from the east and the Allies from the west. On the eve of Germany's collapse the Big Three arranged to meet once more. This meeting, at the Russian seaside resort of Yalta, would have far-reaching consequences, far beyond that of the war still raging in Europe.

10 COLD WARRIOR

A shadow has fallen upon the scenes so lately lighted by the Allied victory. From Stettin in the Baltic to Trieste in the Adriatic, an iron curtain has descended across the Continent.

Winston Churchill at Fulton, Missouri, March 1946[1]

If the Russians go in, will they ever go out?

Franklin Roosevelt on Russia joining the effort to finish the Japanese by attacking Manchuria[2]

HOPES WERE HIGH as the Big Three came to meet at Yalta in 1945. The war in Europe was nearly over, and Hitler's downfall was imminent. There was a chance for the victors to work together for a lasting peace in Europe. As American diplomat Harry Hopkins put it, "this was the dawn of the new day we had all been praying for . . . the first great victory of the peace."3

But it would be a short-lived victory. As united as Roosevelt, Churchill, and Stalin had been in working to defeat Hitler, they were worlds apart in their ideas for a newly liberated Europe. Churchill wanted a free and democratic Europe. Stalin wanted to seal off his borders to the west to assure that the Soviet Union would not be attacked again. That meant extending his sphere of influence into the Eastern European countries surrounding him. Roosevelt, first and foremost, wanted to end the war against Japan, and he was willing to bargain with Stalin to get his help in doing so. With the largest army in Europe, Stalin knew he held the trump card, and he played it for all it was worth.

From the start, Stalin dominated the conference. He insisted the meeting be held on Russian soil because he was too ill to travel. "Short and sturdy, he moved with steady firm steps . . ." wrote American admiral C. E. Olsen, on first seeing Stalin at Yalta. "In spite of his claim to ill health in the preceding seven months, he looked like a most healthy and formidable soldier to deal with now."4

Stalin agreed to send troops to help defeat the Japanese, but at a fearful price. All Soviet prisoners of war and others who had left the country voluntarily were to be returned to the Soviet Union with Allied help. Roosevelt and Churchill must have known that many of these people would be killed or imprisoned by Stalin, but they agreed to the condition anyway. Stalin was allowed to keep his troops in Poland, on the condition that free elections would be held once order was restored.

Within weeks of the conference's end, it was clear that Stalin would not keep his word. His armies remained firmly in power not only in Poland but also in Bulgaria, Hungary, Romania, eastern Germany, Czechoslovakia, and parts of Austria.

"We can't do business with Stalin," Roosevelt told Churchill in late March. "He has broken every one of the promises he made at Yalta."5 Roosevelt was furious, but he was also a very sick man. In mid-April he died of a cerebral hemorrhage. His last message to Churchill was "We must be firm."

In July, a month after the war's end, the three victors—with the new American president Harry Truman replacing Roosevelt—met one last time at Potsdam outside Berlin. Truman knew what he was up against even before the conference began. "Stalin does not and never will fully understand our interest in a free Poland as a matter of principle," U.S. ambassador to Russia Averell Harriman told Truman after meeting with Stalin. "He is a realist in all of his actions, and it is hard for him to appreciate our faith in abstract principles."6

What the three did see eye to eye on was a divided Germany that could never threaten Europe again. They agreed that the defeated nation should be divided into four Allied sectors, governed by an Allied Control Commission. One sector was Soviet; the others, British, French, and American. For Truman and Churchill, there was now no question of working with Stalin for peace; the best they could hope for was to keep the peace by containing him and his influence in Europe.

During the conference, Truman received news that the first atomic bomb had been successfully tested at Alamogordo, New Mexico. This meant that the United States could drop the bomb on Japan and end the war quickly without Stalin's help. At the same time, Truman felt a certain responsibility to share the news of the A-bomb with his wartime ally.

"I casually mentioned to Stalin that we had a new weapon of unusual destructive force," Truman later recalled. "The Russian Premier showed no special interest. All he said was that he was glad to hear it and hoped we would make 'good use of it against the Japanese.' "[7] On August 6, an atomic bomb was dropped on Hiroshima, Japan, from an American B-29. Nagasaki was hit three days later. On September 2, the Japanese officially surrendered to the United States. The war was over.

But the Cold War between Stalin and the West was already under way. This hardening of relationships allowed Stalin to isolate his people from the West and regain the iron grip on the country that had loosened with the Soviet Union's wartime friendship with the West. To unite the Soviet people behind him, Stalin turned to his most effective weapon, propaganda. Almost overnight, the British and Americans went from being friendly allies to capitalist enemies. Stalin's lies and half truths about the West were so effective that several generations of Soviets grew up believing that America was their mortal enemy. It is only fair to point out that the American anti-Communist campaign of the late 1940s and early 1950s was just as indefensible.

In Eastern Europe, Stalin was careful to allow nationalist Communist parties to be established immediately after the war. But within a short time, the national leaders were purged and replaced by Stalinists. "This is certainly not the Liberated Europe we fought to build up," Churchill said in his famous "Iron Curtain" speech in Fulton, Missouri. "Nor is it one which contains the essentials of permanent peace."[8]

To counter Stalin's aggression in Eastern Europe, Truman instituted the Truman Doctrine in 1947 and offered aid to any country that resisted a Communist takeover. The subsequent Marshall Plan gave billions of U.S. dollars to non-Communist countries to rebuild themselves after the destruction of the war.

In June 1948, Stalin struck back with his most audacious move of the postwar era. The city of Berlin, like Germany itself, had been divided into zones occupied by the French, British, Americans, and Soviets, although the city was deep in East Germany. Stalin decided to force the Western Allies to leave Berlin by blockading the city. He didn't think the Allies would risk war by coming to the city's aid, but he didn't count on feisty Harry Truman. The American president publicly called Stalin an "old SOB" and ordered an airlift to drop supplies into the isolated city.

The American airlift brought in over two million tons of supplies to West Berlin. Stalin admitted defeat and called off the blockade within a year. It was a victory for the West, but one that taught them an important lesson. In April 1949, twelve Western democracies, including the United States and Britain, formed the North Atlantic Treaty Organization (NATO). Each member vowed to go to war if any one of them were to be attacked. It was the first such treaty the United States had ever signed.

The year 1948 was a bad one for Stalin. He not only faced humiliation from the West but he also had trouble right in his own backyard. Of the leaders in the Communist bloc, the most independent-minded was Josip Broz, better known as Tito. Tito, a veteran Communist, seized power in Yugoslavia in 1945. He resisted Stalin's interference with his government and would not allow the Soviet Union to rob his country of its resources. No Communist leader in or out of the Soviet Union had ever stood up to Stalin and lived to boast about it. "I will shake my little finger and there will be no more Tito," Stalin told Khrushchev.9 But even Stalin's whole fist wasn't enough to remove Tito from power. Stalin attempted an economic blockade of Yugoslavia and even sent teams of assassins to kill the rebellious leader, all to no avail. Tito had not only the full support of the Yugoslav people but the support of the West, who saw him as a crack in Stalin's Iron Curtain.

In a remarkable letter not discovered until after Stalin's death, Tito gave this response to the Soviet leader's threats: "Comrade Stalin, if this does not stop, I will send one man to Moscow and there will be no need to send another."10 Stalin left Tito pretty much alone after that, and the Yugoslav leader remained in power until his death in 1980.

Tito's independence from Stalin was a model for another young Communist leader. In 1949, Mao Ze-dong won the long civil war against nationalist leader Chiang Kai-shek and declared China a Communist republic. Stalin longed to add the People's Republic of China to his growing empire, but Mao resisted. In truth, Stalin had done little to help Mao in his struggle, and the Chinese felt they owed him nothing in return. When Mao visited Moscow in 1949, Stalin gave him a pittance in aid, and the two men signed a Sino-Soviet pact to keep some semblance of peace between them. If Stalin couldn't win over the Chinese, he was determined to see that the West didn't make friends with them either. He looked for a way to create a lasting enmity between the United States and China. The Korean War, which he helped start in 1950, was the answer to his prayers.

Marshall Tito, Yugoslavia's Communist leader (right) refused to let his country become a mere Soviet satellite after World War II, much to Stalin's chagrin. Tito's rebellion would serve as a dangerous model for Hungary and later Czechoslovakia, whose attempts to break with Stalinism would be quickly crushed.

Korea, like Germany, was divided against itself after the war. The northern part of the country, the Communist-run Democratic People's Republic, came under Soviet influence. The Republic of Korea in the south was supported by the United States. With a little encouragement from Stalin, the North Koreans invaded South Korea in hopes of taking it over. Stalin's plan was to entangle China in the subsequent war and weaken it. Again, he miscalculated the West's response. The United Nations condemned the North Korean invasion and a peacekeeping force of sixteen nations sent troops to Korea. When the North Koreans refused to accept the surrender demands of the U.S. commander, General Douglas MacArthur, American troops invaded North Korea. Fearing the Americans would cross the nearby Chinese border, Mao sent a million Chinese troops to help the North Koreans.*

Stalin sent aid and advisors but no troops into North Korea, and the Soviet Union remained at peace. But its aging dictator would find little personal peace in the few years remaining to him.

---

* The war finally ended in 1953, only months after Stalin's death, at a cost of close to three million lives. After all the fighting, the border between North and South Korea remained nearly where it had been before the war. Stalin had succeeded in driving an iron wedge between the United States and China that would remain in place for decades. However, China emerged from the Korean War stronger than ever before.

11 TYRANT'S TWILIGHT

I'm finished. I trust no one, not even myself.

Stalin to himself, overheard by Khrushchev, 1951[1]

He's going to wipe us all out.

Beria to a party friend, early 1953[2]

N DECEMBER 21, 1949, Stalin celebrated his seventieth birthday. It was an occasion of international note. Lavish gifts flooded into the Kremlin from all over the world. There were so many birthday presents that the government created a museum in Stalin's hometown of Gori to display them all. In Moscow's Red Square, the day was marked with military parades and thundering gun salutes. The evening climaxed with a huge portrait of Stalin suspended from a balloon and illuminated by searchlights. People went home from the festivities clutching tiny plaster statues of their leader, mass-produced for the occasion. Unlike the holy men of the church, Stalin had achieved sainthood while still alive.

But for all his power and popularity, Stalin was not a happy man. NATO had frustrated his schemes to take over Greece and Turkey; Tito was firmly entrenched in Yugoslavia; and Mao, his guest during the birthday celebration, would no more take orders from Stalin than he would from President Truman. Like Hitler's, Stalin's dream of world domination was rapidly fading.

Shades of mortality were descending on the man of steel. His aging body suffered from a host of maladies. He had arthritis, sciatica, high blood pressure, and heart trouble. His withered left arm, always a problem, now throbbed constantly with pain. Although he had abused his health for decades with tobacco, alcohol, and overeating, Stalin clung desperately to the legend of Georgian longevity, pointing to those of his countrymen who had lived to be a hundred or more.

There was no comfort in his personal life in these declining years. Since his second wife's death in 1932, he had had no meaningful relationship with a woman. Of his three children, Yakov was dead, Vasily was a hopeless alcoholic, and Svetlana an ingrate who had further angered her father by marrying a Jew. The idyllic days of the loving father and little daughter were long gone. As Svetlana grew to womanhood and became her own person, Stalin lost interest in her. He rarely saw her anymore. When she asked for his permission to marry, he told her gruffly, "To hell with you, do what you like."

His eight grandchildren fared no better. He flatly refused to see five of them because they were part Jewish.* The rest of his family and in-laws were either dead or in prison by his own order.

As for his colleagues and friends, they were reduced to the role of lackeys and toadies. The moral degradation of Stalin's twilight years can be summed up in his late-night dinners with his inner circle. The menu consisted of roast beef and large quantities of vodka drunk in endless toasts to Stalin. Stalin's only pleasure, other than the late-night double features that would follow, was presiding over humiliating games and childish pranks at the expense of his guests. One time they had to guess how many degrees below zero the temperature was outside. Then they were forced to drink a glass of vodka for each degree by which they had missed. Other times Stalin would have a ripe tomato placed on a man's chair before he sat down or have salt sprinkled in the wine. A NKVD man was assigned to clean up after each guest and then see him safely home.

But these diversions could not fill the vast void of the dictator's lonely life. More and more, Stalin seemed preoccupied about his place in history. The first of sixteen volumes of Stalin's *Collected Works*, edited by himself, appeared in 1949. In the summer of 1950 he began work

* Yakov, like Svetlana, married a Jew.

In the last years of his reign, Stalin's image was pervasive throughout the Soviet bloc. He was particularly fond of large, monumental statues of himself like this one in Bucharest, Romania. Most of these statues were torn down during the period of "destalinization" in the late 1950s.

on the "Great Stalinist Plan for Remaking Nature," which involved ambitious projects of bridge and canal construction, some of which were never completed.

In his final days, Stalin went to great pains to portray himself as a man of peace. On the final day of the 19th Congress of the Soviet Union in October 1952 he delivered what would be his last speech. "Long live peace among nations!" he said in closing. "Down with the warmongers!"[3]

But beneath the mellowing facade, Stalin had lost none of his blood lust. As a new year dawned, the old man was quietly engineering his last purge. On January 13, 1953, seven highly respected Kremlin doctors were accused of conspiring to murder a number of government officials who had been under their care, including two former Politburo members.

Stalin had never liked doctors. Only a short time before, he had had his own personal doctor of many years arrested as a spy. But there was a deeper, more disturbing pattern that emerged from the "Doctors' Plot." Five of the seven accused doctors were Jewish. Stalin's anti-Semitism was well known, if less well publicized than Hitler's. Many men in the Kremlin were uneasy, and for good reason. Beria was part Jewish and had even created a Jewish museum, the first of its kind in the Soviet Union. Khrushchev's daughter had married a Jewish journalist. In one master stroke, it looked as if Stalin was going to wipe out all his potential rivals and the Jews. As the weeks passed, hundreds of Jews were arrested and "persuaded" by the NKVD to confess to being part of this imagined conspiracy, instigated, according to Stalin, by the British and Americans.

The country held its breath, waiting for the ax to fall. But it never did. On March 1, Stalin treated himself to a steam bath, a foolhardy thing for a man of his age and poor health to do. The next day Stalin was alone in his dacha when a blood vessel burst in his brain. Hours later, his guards found him lying on the carpet, unable to talk, his right side paralyzed. Afraid to move their stricken leader, his top aides had him placed in his own bed and kept vigil by his side as a battery of doctors tried to save him with leeches and an array of other questionable treatments.

The Central Committee kept Stalin's illness a secret for three days, as his condition grew more and more hopeless. The seventy-three-year-old man was slowly losing consciousness from the bleeding in his brain. Here is how Svetlana described her father's final moments:

> *The death agony was horrible. He literally choked to death as we watched. At what seemed like the very last moment he suddenly opened his eyes and cast a glance over everyone in the room. It was a terrible glance, insane or perhaps angry and full of the fear of death and the unfamiliar faces of the doctors bent over him. . . . Then something incomprehensible and awesome happened that to this day I can't forget and don't understand. He suddenly lifted his left hand as though he were pointing to something above and bringing down a curse on us all. The gesture was incomprehensible and full of menace, and no one could say to whom or at what it might be directed. The next moment, after a final effort, the spirit wrenched itself free of the flesh.*[4]

"The heart of the comrade-in-arms and continuer of genius of Lenin's cause, of the wise leader and teacher of the Communist Party and the Soviet Union, has ceased to

A grim-faced group of Stalin aides carries their leader's coffin to its resting place beside Lenin. In front on the left is Lavrenty Beria, Stalin's chief of secret police. Beria hoped to succeed Stalin, but was outmaneuvered by Khrushchev and his allies and executed before the year was out.

beat," the announcer on Soviet state radio told the world the morning after Stalin died.[5] Death had finally done what Lenin, Hitler, and a host of others had been unable to do. It had finally purged the world of Joseph Stalin.

The Father of All the Russias lay in state for three days while the Communist world mourned his passing. Most living Soviets could not remember a time he had not been in power. They had gone beyond loving or hating Stalin. He was a force of nature, an omnipresence whose very name and image had become synonymous with the Soviet Union. Many sincerely mourned his passing, many others breathed a sigh of relief, and some rejoiced. "I have been here for 19 years and this is the first good news I have had," crowed one anonymous prisoner in the gulag.[6]

The funeral took place on March 9. In a coffin draped in black and red silk, Stalin, the pockmarks gone from his face under the mortician's skillful hand, was carried to rest beside Lenin in the Kremlin mausoleum.

The massive crowd pressed in as the funeral procession passed through Red Square. "The crush turned into a monstrous whirlpool," recalled poet Yevgeny Yevtushenko, who was there. "I felt I was treading on something soft. It was a human body."[7] Between 500 and 1,500 people perished in the frenzy that followed. They must be counted as Stalin's last victims.

12

THE LONG, DARK LEGACY

*Stalin looked to the czarist
past for cues to present
policy. He found them in
the centuries-old heritage
of a powerful, centralized,
bureaucratic state.*

Robert C. Tucker[1]

IN HIS REMARKABLE BOOK *The Red Monarch: Scenes from the Life of Stalin*, Russian author Yuri Krotkov mixes fact and fiction to create a portrait of Stalin more true than that found in most biographies. In one memorable sketch, Krotkov retells Stalin's final illness in the words of his head of security. The narrator comically describes Beria, Khrushchev, and the other members of the Central Committee standing outside Stalin's locked door nervously debating whether to break in or wait, fearing the dictator might only be sleeping. Once they have broken in and found their stricken leader, they immediately begin plotting who will succeed him.

In the struggle for power, Beria was the first loser. Stalin's chief of police had too many enemies. Khrushchev, supported by Premier Georgi Malenkov and former foreign minister Molotov, had Beria arrested and shot two days after what would have been Stalin's seventy-fourth birthday. Khrushchev eventually emerged as supreme leader, but except for Beria, he dealt mercifully with his rivals and restricted the power of the NKVD, soon to be renamed the KGB.

Khrushchev's 1956 denunciation of Stalin and his program of "destalinization" was a selective purge. Many of Stalin's crimes went unnamed, especially those in which Khrushchev and his colleagues had played a part. While the man Stalin was vilified, his larger legacy was left untouched. The statues and pictures were gone, but Stalin's greatest monument—the bureaucratic state he built—remained intact for another three decades.

Khrushchev, with good intentions, tinkered with the machinery. He tried to improve the lot of the average

Soviet by increasing production of consumer goods and foodstuffs. He built bridges of friendship with the West and even visited the United States. Yet, he also remained faithful to Stalinism by keeping firm control over the Eastern Soviet bloc and continuing to escalate the nuclear arms race with the West. Khrushchev's economic policies, however well intended, largely failed. When he lost China's never-secure friendship by becoming too friendly with the West, it was the last straw. He was quietly ousted by the other members of the Politburo and sent into retirement in 1964.

Leonid Brezhnev, Khrushchev's top lieutenant, took over power. In the eighteen years until his death in 1982, Brezhnev oversaw the final stage of Stalinism and its ultimate failure. The massive Soviet bureaucracy that kept the privileged elite in power began to stagnate. Corruption ran rampant, the economy calcified, and the soul of the Soviet Union sickened as the people lost all hope of a better day under communism. For the Soviet people, disillusionment led to alcoholism, soaring divorce rates, and an alarming mortality rate. As historian Robert C. Tucker has written, Brezhnev's reign "bequeathed a swollen state and a spent society."[2]

Mikhail Gorbachev, who came to power in 1985, was a new breed of Soviet leader. He tried to revitalize a dying society with economic freedom and new personal liberties. But Stalin's Russia was beyond reforming. The only way it could be changed was to tear down the entire rotting edifice. Gorbachev, who hoped to change communism for the better, ended up presiding over its demise.

As new revelations about his life and crimes emerged from the unlocked files of his nation's archives, Stalin loomed as large in the world's collective memory as he ever did in life. The evidence was irrefutable. No better personification of pure evil could be found in modern times. In his quarter century in power, Stalin murdered as many as 40 million people—most of them his own countrymen.

But it would be historically wrong to see Stalin as an aberration in Russian history. His paranoia, his fear of foreign invasion, and his desire for a closed society under his absolute control, were all part of a long tradition going back to the first czars. It would be equally wrong to see Stalin as the spoiler of Lenin's Bolshevik state. After all, it was that same Bolshevik system that nurtured Stalin and allowed him to rise to the top. Without Lenin, Stalin would never have existed.

As for Stalin's disastrous attempts to appease Hitler before World War II, they too must be put in historical context. All of Europe—including Britain under Churchill's predecessor, Neville Chamberlain—sought to appease Hitler and avoid war. Although none took as ignominious a path as the Soviet-Nazi nonaggression pact, they all in their way must share some of the responsibility for Hitler's rise. Some historians have even argued that the Cold War was as much Truman's fault as Stalin's. They have claimed that the Marshall Plan's refusal to help the Soviet Union to rebuild after World War II pushed Stalin into an aggressive position and hastened the dropping of the Iron Curtain.

None of these qualifications can begin to excuse Stalin's black crimes against humanity. Yet for all his evil, one must come to grips with the fact that Stalin did do some good. He wrenched an antiquated society out of the past and dragged it into the twentieth century. He transformed Russia from a land of peasant farmers into an industrial

Like one of Russia's czars of old, Stalin bent his country and its people to his will. During his long reign he transformed Russia from a backward land into a world power, but at the terrible cost of at least 50 million lives.

giant, a world superpower whose empire rivaled any in history. The price paid for these advances in terms of human suffering is incalculable. Stalin's dark legacy is both horrible and awesome. We can hate Stalin, but we cannot ignore him. For good or ill, he changed the world we live in as much as any human being in the twentieth century.

And what of the country he left behind? By the 1990s the Soviet Union had become only a shadow of its former self. The Soviet republics, renamed the Commonwealth of Independent States (CIS), and their Eastern European satellites went their separate ways. Some, including Yugoslavia, Czechoslovakia, and Stalin's own Georgia, found that freedom from communism only unleashed other age-old evils of civil strife.

Boris Yeltsin, who became Russia's new leader in 1991, struggled to remake his land into a democratic country. But the ghost of Stalin continued to linger in the Kremlin air. As discontent over the floundering economy rose, some yearned for a return to the old order, however harsh. Neo-Stalinists made pilgrimages to his hometown of Gori, the only place in Russia where Stalin was still openly venerated. And letters like this one appeared periodically in local newspapers:

> *Yes, Stalin was responsible for repressions, but Khrushchev and Brezhnev are responsible for decay of faith in our just cause. So, what's worse—to lose several million people, or to have tens of millions who've lost moral orientation? Russia needs an iron hand for the life span of another generation! Stalin signifies a fantastical sense of the Motherland and a punitive sword!*[3]

For all the warped nostalgia some have for the Stalin years, it is hard to imagine that many people would like to see the "punitive sword" unsheathed again. But the terrible question remains. If reforms fail and democracy does not take root in the stony soil of the former Soviet Union, will another Stalin arise to take charge? We can only hope that this will not happen. May Stalin, the most terrible czar of Russia, remain its last.

HRONOLOGY

(Old Style dates are used prior to February 1918, when the New Style, or Western, calendar came into use. Old Style dates are twelve days behind the New Style in the nineteenth century and thirteen days behind in the twentieth.)

1879	Iosif Vissarionovich Dzhugashvili (Stalin) is born in Gori, a village in Georgia, Russia (December 21)
1894	Enters Tbilisi Theological Seminary to study for the priesthood
1899	Expelled from the seminary for missing exams; already committed to revolutionary cause
1900	Makes first public speech at a demonstration near Tbilisi (April 23)
1901	First articles published in revolutionary journal *Brdzola*
1902	Arrested for first time for revolutionary activities in Batum (April 18)
1903	Exiled to Siberia for the first of six times; escapes the following January
1904	Marries Ekaterina Svanidze, a Georgian girl
1905	Bloody Sunday in St. Petersburg begins an unsuccessful people's revolution (January 22)

	Stalin attends revolutionary conference in Finland and meets Lenin for the first time (December 25–30)
1906	Meets Lenin again at Social Democratic Congress in Stockholm, Sweden (April)
1907	Wife dies (October)
1908–1912	In exile or prison most of this period
1912	Chosen by Lenin as a member of the Central Committee of the Bolshevik party (February)
	Helps to found Bolshevik newspaper *Pravda* (April)
1913	Arrested and exiled to Siberia for the last time
1914	World War I begins
1917	Czar Nicholas II resigns and a provisional government takes power in first phase of Russian Revolution (February, March)
	Bolsheviks take over St. Petersburg and later the country in second phase of Revolution (October, November)
1918–1921	Civil war is waged between the Reds (Communists) and Whites (non-Communists)
1922	Stalin, previously commissar of nationalities, is appointed general secretary of the Central Committee
1924	Lenin dies (January 21)
	Troika of Stalin, Kamenev, and Zinoviev takes power
1925	Stalin shifts his loyalty to Bukharin and party conservatives; Kamenev, Zinoviev, and Trotsky are expelled from the Politburo
1929	Stalin is sole leader of Soviet Union as his fiftieth birthday is celebrated; Trotsky goes into exile
1930–1933	Kulaks are eliminated; resistance to collectivization by peasant farmers leads to widespread famine
1932	Stalin's second wife, Nadezhda Alliluyeva, dies, probably a suicide (November 7)
1934	Sergei Kirov, Leningrad party boss, is assassinated

1936–1938	Zinoviev, Kamenev, Bukharin, and other leading Bolsheviks are implicated in Kirov's death, tried in three show trials, and executed along with millions of other Russians during Stalin's reign of terror
1939	Nonaggression pact signed between Soviet Union and Nazi Germany (August 23) Hitler invades Poland, starting World War II (September 1) Stalin goes to war with Finland (November 30)
1941	Germany invades Russia (June 22)
1942–1943	The Battle of Stalingrad ends in a decisive victory for the Russians
1943	The Big Three—Stalin, Churchill, and Roosevelt—meet in Teheran, Iran, to plan their strategy against Hitler (November 28–December 1)
1945	Big Three meet at Yalta (February 3–11) War ends in Europe with Hitler's defeat; Potsdam Conference held (July) Japan surrenders after United States drops atomic bombs on Hiroshima and Nagasaki (September 2)
1946–1947	Stalin gradually takes over eight Eastern European countries; the Cold War begins
1948	Stalin breaks off diplomatic relations with rebellious Communist leader Tito of Yugoslavia
1949	Mao Ze-dong, Communist leader of China, visits Stalin during his seventieth birthday celebration
1950	The Korean War begins, with Stalin supporting the Communists in North Korea
1953	The "Doctors' Plot" is revealed, foreshadowing a new purge (January) Stalin dies of a cerebral hemorrhage (March 5)
1956	Khrushchev denounces Stalin at the 20th Party Congress; "destalinization" begins
1961	Stalin's body is removed from Lenin's mausoleum and buried near the Kremlin wall (October 31)

^OTES

Chapter One
1. Burt Hirschfeld, *Khrushchev* (New York: Hawthorn Books, 1968), p. 129.
2. Robert Payne, *The Rise and Fall of Stalin* (New York: Simon & Schuster, 1965), pp. 712–713.
3. Ibid. p. 713.

Chapter Two
1. *Current Biography Yearbook 1942* (New York: H. W. Wilson Co., 1942), pp. 790–791.
2. Payne, p. 45.
3. Ibid. p. 47.
4. Ibid. p. 57.

Chapter Three
1. Payne, p. 95.
2. Ibid. p. 99.
3. Albert Marrin, *Stalin: Russia's Man of Steel* (New York: Viking, 1988), p. 34.
4. Payne, p. 107.

Chapter Four
1. Payne, p. 128.
2. Ibid. p. 101.
3. Marrin, p. 38.
4. Payne, p. 136.

5. Ibid. p. 163.
6. Ibid. p. 166.

Chapter Five
1. Payne, p. 167.
2. Marrin, p. 65.
3. Marrin, pp. 67–68.

Chapter Six
1. Payne, p. 369.
2. Ibid. p. 369.
3. Ibid. p. 344.
4. Ibid. p. 347.
5. Marrin, p. 71.
6. Payne, p. 369.
7. Ibid. p. 371.

Chapter Seven
1. Marrin, p. 86.
2. Ibid. p. 92.
3. Janet Caulkins, *Joseph Stalin* (New York: Franklin Watts, 1990), p. 80.
4. Payne, p. 630.

Chapter Eight
1. Payne, p. 468.
2. Graham Yost, *The KGB* (New York: Facts on File, 1989), p. 47.
3. Payne, p. 465.
4. Ibid. p. 506.
5. Marrin, p. 134.
6. William Harlan Hale, "The Road to Yalta," *American Heritage*, June 1961, p. 39.
7. Caulkins, p. 101.
8. Payne, p. 470.
9. Nikita Khrushchev, "Khrushchev's Secret Tapes," *Time*, October 1, 1990, pp. 69–70.
10. Svetlana Alliluyeva, *Twenty Letters to a Friend* (New York: Harper & Row, 1967), p. 150.

Chapter Nine
1. Eugene H. Methvin, "The Unquiet Ghosts of Stalin's Victims," *The National Review*, September 1, 1989, p. 25.
2. Marrin, epigram.
3. Ibid. p. 155.
4. Ibid. p. 184.
5. Caulkins, p. 121.

Chapter Ten
1. Marrin, p. 221.
2. Charles L. Mee, Jr., W. Averell Harriman, and Elie Abel, "Who Started the Cold War?" *American Heritage*, August 1977, p. 18.
3. Ibid. p. 84.
4. Admiral C. E. Olsen, "Full House at Yalta," *American Heritage*, June 1972, p. 21.
5. Mee, Harriman, and Abel, p. 17.
6. Ibid. pp. 11–12.
7. Ibid. p. 14.
8. Ibid. p. 15.
9. Payne, p. 643.
10. Marrin, p. 224.

Chapter Eleven
1. Marrin, p. 229.
2. Ibid. p. 230.
3. Payne, p. 662.
4. Alliluyeva, p. 10.
5. Payne, p. 682.
6. Marrin, p. 233.
7. Payne, p. 685.

Chapter Twelve
1. Robert C. Tucker, "Giving Up the Ghost," *The New Republic*, October 17, 1988, p. 33.
2. Tucker, "The Last Leninist," *The New York Times*, December 29, 1991.
3. G. Turetsky, quoted by Robert C. Tucker in *The New Republic*, p. 20.

BIBLIOGRAPHY

Alliluyeva, Svetlana. *Twenty Letters to a Friend*. New York: Harper & Row, 1967. (Stalin's daughter's intimate and intriguing recollections of her father.)

Caulkins, Janet. *Joseph Stalin*. New York: Franklin Watts, 1990. (A young adult biography.)

Conquest, Robert. *Stalin: Breaker of Nations*. New York: Viking, 1991. (One of the most up-to-date biographies on the dictator by a leading authority on the Stalin years.)

DeJonge, Alex. *Stalin and the Shaping of the Soviet Union*. New York: William Morrow, 1986. (DeJonge's scholarship is impressive, but his view of Stalin as a ruthless corporate executive is hard to swallow.)

Khrushchev, Nikita. *Khrushchev Remembers*. Boston: Little, Brown and Co., 1970, 1974, and 1990. (Khrushchev's three volumes of memoirs offer a fascinating portrait of Stalin as seen by one of his top lieutenants.)

Krotkov, Yuri. *The Red Monarch: Scenes from the Life of Stalin*. New York: W. W. Norton, 1979. (This fictionalized collection of stories by a Russian writer who lived under Stalinism gets closer to the truth about Stalin than a dozen biographies.)

Marrin, Albert. *Stalin: Russia's Man of Steel.* New York: Viking, 1988. (A young adult biography, particularly good on the World War II period.)

Payne, Robert. *The Rise and Fall of Stalin.* New York: Simon & Schuster, 1965. (This is an immensely readable and well-written popular biography.)

Rybakov, Anatoli. *Children of the Arbat.* New York: Dell, 1988. (An epic autobiographical novel set in the pre-terror thirties. Rybakov interweaves the story of a young Muscovite's arrest and exile with scenes from Stalin's life.)

INDEX

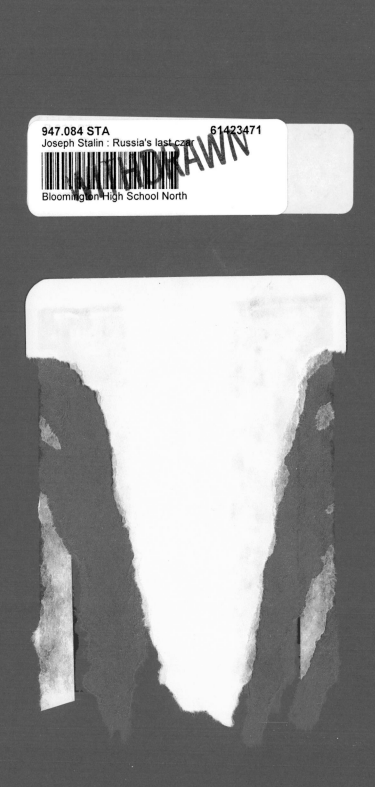